BIBLE DIFFICULTIES

AN EXAMINATION OF PASSAGES OF THE BIBLE ALLEGED TO BE IRRECONCILABLE WITH ITS INSPIRATION

BY

W. ARNDT

PROFESSOR OF HERMENEUTICS AND NEW TESTAMENT EXEGESIS
AT CONCORDIA SEMINARY, ST. LOUIS, MO.

CONCORDIA PUBLISHING HOUSE - ST. LOUIS, MO.

EIGHTH PRINTING
1971

PRINTED IN U. S. A.

ISBN   0-570-03120-6

Foreword

There is nothing surprising in the fact that there are "Bible difficulties" or that Christian scholars should feel moved to write books with titles like *Bible Difficulties*. There is no other book so old, so remote from us in time and culture, and so varied in form and content that is read, and read with profit, by so many people not particularly well equipped to deal with ancient documents. The surprising thing is, not that there are difficulties but that there are so many men and women of good will who learn to read the record of God's people and God's Son without serious difficulty and can hear in its words the voice of the Good Shepherd whom they know and can trust in life and in the valley of the shadow of death.

It was for readers of this sort that Dr. Arndt originally wrote this book. He wrote in the closing words of his preface: "To *our . . . Savior. . .* the fortunes of this book are entrusted. May it please Him to use it, even if only in a small measure, for the furtherance of the cause of His holy Gospel, which is the power of God unto salvation to every one that believeth!" He was not attempting to silence the strident voices, rational or rebellious, which strive to howl down the voice of the Good Shepherd and keep it from reaching the ears of those who know that without Him they are like sheep gone astray. He wrote for people who call Jesus Savior, and his aim was a more modest one: to brush away the singing gnats that irritate and distract those intent upon listening to the Shepherd's voice. Over the 38 years since its first publication his book has performed its intended service faithfully and well, and it is being reissued in the hope and with the prayer that its genial and saintly author cherished and uttered when he first sent the book on its way.

MARTIN H. FRANZMANN

Cambridge, England
Jan. 7, 1971

Contents

PART ONE

Some General Considerations

ARE THERE DIFFICULT PASSAGES IN THE SCRIPTURES?

It might seem to one or the other of my readers that the title of this book casts an unwarranted reflection on our Holy Book and that we should not speak of difficult passages in the Bible. If it is the Word of God given to lead us to salvation, then it must be without blemish, clear and intelligible, and to say that there are difficulties in it apparently does not agree with its divine origin and with its exalted character as our one and only guide to heavenly life. Let those who think and speak thus be assured that it is not the object of this little book to deny the divineness and the clearness and intelligibility of the Scriptures.

We must not forget, however, that the Bible itself declares that there are some things in it which are difficult to understand. Let the reader open his copy of the Scriptures at 2 Pet. 3:16 and see what St. Peter says about the Epistles of St. Paul. He states that in them there are "some things hard to be understood, which they that are unlearned and unstable wrest, as they do also the other Scriptures, unto their own destruction." There is here the unequivocal declaration that in the Epistles of St. Paul some things are hard to be understood, and that settles the question for us. The Apostle does not say that all or many things in St. Paul's writings present difficulties. He is merely referring to some things. Now, if there are some things in St. Paul's letters that can be designated as difficult, it is not improbable that there are some things in the other sections of the Bible, too, which are not quite easy of comprehension.

Our experience bears this out. The Bible reader will now and then come upon a verse or paragraph which makes him ask: What meaneth this? Like the eunuch reading the Prophet Isaiah, Acts 8:27 ff., he will be puzzled by the language of the sacred writers. The existence of numerous commentaries on the Scriptures, written by devout Christian men, confirms the view that here and there a difficult passage appears in the Bible; for though it is not the sole purpose of commentaries to explain difficulties, this is at least one of their avowed objects.

The difficulties which are pointed to in the Bible by its friends and its foes are of many sorts and colors. The great majority of them are entirely of man's own making and will vanish when prayerfully studied. A few are due to our inability to understand the language of the holy writers in the respective passages; others must be attributed to our ignorance of historical, geographical, economic, and social conditions at the time when the books of the Bible were written. Some people maintain that they find difficulties in the Scriptures on moral grounds, thinking there are things in them which are objectionable and harmful. Others again believe that they have found instances where science and the Bible clash and the statements of the latter are not tenable.

Often passages are referred to with the assertion that they contradict each other, and not a few people say that here there are stumbling blocks for them. It is my intention to discuss the chief difficulties which, people say, they encounter in their Bible reading, with the exception of seeming contradictions which I treated in a little book *Does the Bible Contradict Itself?* This book was likewise published by Concordia Publishing House, St. Louis, Mo., and those that wish to make a study of alleged discrepancies in the Scriptures I should like to refer to this treatise. Before taking up particular passages, we have to see what must be our attitude toward the Bible in general. In the first place, the doctrine that the Bible is inspired will have to be looked at.

THE BIBLE DOCTRINE OF INSPIRATION

Among the many great subjects which the Bible discusses is its own nature, origin, and purpose. Just as the Scriptures tell us about Christ the God-Man and Savior, so they tell us about themselves. Therefore, in speaking of the inspiration of the Scriptures, we are treating one of the doctrines of Holy Writ. Whether this doctrine is true or not is, of course, a separate question, which we shall touch on by and by; but for the present let us fix our attention on the thought that the Bible has given us teaching on itself. Evidently it behooves us to see what this teaching is. It cannot be my object here to present an exhaustive treatment, but merely to mention some points that appear to me most important and conclusive.

In considering what the Bible has to say about its origin, we had best at once go to the New Testament. One cannot read the New Testament with any degree of care without observing that it offers clear and striking testimony as to the character of the Old Testament. Let us think of what Jesus, our Lord, has to say about it. When He is tempted by the devil, Matt. 4:1 ff., He vanquishes the foe by means of quotations from the Scriptures. We remember, of course, that at the time of His sojourn among men the Old Testament was the only part of the Scriptures in existence. "It is written," He says three times. A majestic, powerful declaration! It makes the Old Testament Scriptures a divine norm, standard, and authority. Jesus does not submit these Old Testament texts for discussion, but merely to show Satan that he is wrong. If we had nothing else from the lips of Jesus, this brief statement alone would indicate that the Old Testament was regarded by Him as possessing divine authority.

Another passage is Matt. 22:43, where Jesus, quoting the 110th Psalm, says: "How doth David in Spirit call Him [that is, the Messiah] Lord?" In referring to this holy song of David, Jesus declares that David produced it in Spirit, that is, by the Spirit, namely, the Spirit of God.

Well known are the words of Jesus recorded John 10:35: "The Scriptures cannot be broken." It is a statement which must be studied in its connection. The Jews had accused Jesus of blasphemy because He had said that He and the Father are one, ascribing deity to Himself. Then He points out to them that in their own Holy Book, the Old Testament, the title "gods" was applied to men who were receiving the Word of God, namely, the judges of Israel. The passage He alludes to is Ps. 82:6: "I have said: Ye are gods and all of you are children of the Most High." The argument of Jesus runs thus: God Himself gave the judges of Israel the exalted title "gods," and that is an appellation which no one can take from them because the Scripture cannot be broken, because it is of inviolate and absolute authority; how much less, then, should anybody be offended when He who had come from the bosom of the Father above called Himself the Son of God! "The Scripture cannot be broken" — Olshausen is right when he in his commentary interprets these words of Jesus to mean that "the Scripture, as the expressed will of the unchangeable God, is itself unchangeable and indissoluble." God has spoken, and His Word you cannot set aside, thus we might paraphrase this famous saying of our Lord. It, then, implies quite distinctly the divine origin and authority of the Scriptures. And what makes this saying of Jesus particularly impressive is that it pertains to one word, or expression, in the Old Testament, not to a doctrine or a general truth. It teaches that not even single terms employed in the Scriptures can be disregarded, be their function ever so subordinate.

2 Timothy 3:16

One of the chief passages for us to cite here is 2 Tim. 3:16: "All Scripture is given by inspiration of God and is profitable for doctrine, for reproof, for correction, for instruction in righteousness." It is the text from which the term "inspiration" has been derived. According to the connection, St. Paul has in mind the Old Testament Scriptures, which Timothy had known from a child. (Cf. v. 15.) In my opinion the Revised Version, agreeing with Luther, gives the correct translation of the passage, rendering it: "Every Scripture inspired of God is also profitable for teaching, for reproof, for correction, for instruction which is in righteousness." The Apostle here presents teaching on the origin of the Scriptures, which he has spoken of in the preceding verse. There he has given them the attribute "holy." Here he calls them "inspired of God." Literally translated, this term would read: God-breathed. It is a beautiful figure which he uses, signifying that just as our breath proceeds from us, so the Scriptures have come from God.

If the objection is made that Paul, according to the translation of the Revised Version, does not ascribe this quality to all the Scriptures, but that his meaning is: If a Scripture is inspired of God, then it is likewise profitable, etc., and that hence we are not justified in basing on this passage our doctrine of the inspiration of the Bible or any part of it, I reply that Paul certainly does not wish to make merely a hypothetical statement. On the contrary, when he follows up his remark on the power of the Holy Scriptures in v. 15 with the declaration that every God-breathed Scripture is also profitable for doctrine, etc., the unbiased reader at once perceives that the Apostle is alluding to the very writings which he has spoken of before in such high terms and that he merely varies the expression, using "God-breathed" instead of "holy." Every such God-breathed Scripture as I have made mention of is also profitable for doctrine, etc., — thus his meaning might fairly be given.

2 PETER 1:21

St. Peter makes a noteworthy statement about the holy penmen of God of the Old Testament when he says, 2 Pet. 1:21: "Holy men of God spake as they were moved by the Holy Ghost." The preceding verse shows that the Apostle is discussing the Holy Scriptures ("knowing this first, that no prophecy of the Scripture is of any private interpretation," v. 20). How did these Holy Scriptures originate? Holy men of God spoke, but they spoke as the Spirit of God moved them. What they said was in a sense their own product, and yet we have to say that it was not their own product, but the Word of the Holy Spirit.

In the Epistle to the Hebrews several Old Testament passages are directly ascribed to the Holy Spirit as Author. Thus when Ps. 95:7 is quoted, the passage is introduced by the words "As the Holy Ghost saith," Heb. 3:7. Cp. also Heb. 10:15. Many more passages of like tenor could here be adduced; but I think that those which I have pointed to will suffice to show that the Old Testament writings are in the New Testament said to owe their origin to God, particularly to the Holy Spirit.

STATUS OF THE NEW TESTAMENT

Now, what of the New Testament? About it, too, we have Scripture declarations showing that it is of divine origin. As the titles of the various books indicate, it came from the pens of Apostles and assistants of Apostles. But these men were endowed with the Holy Spirit and were made the infallible teachers of the Church. When they spoke and wrote, it was really the Spirit of God who was speaking and writing. In proof of this important, far-reaching statement we can point to John 14:26: "But the

Comforter, which is the Holy Ghost, whom the Father will send in My name, He shall teach you all things and bring all things to your remembrance, whatsoever I have said unto you." Matt. 10:20: "For it is not ye that speak, but the Spirit of your Father which speaketh in you." 1 Cor. 2:13: "Which things also we speak, not in the words which man's wisdom teacheth, but which the Holy Ghost teacheth, comparing spiritual things with spiritual."

Let the reader furthermore remember that the Christian Church, according to the words of St. Paul, Eph. 2:20, is built not only on the Prophets, but likewise on the Apostles; in fact, the latter are mentioned first. They rank with the inspired Prophets of old, their writings being as much God-breathed as those of Moses and Isaiah. Cf. 2 Pet. 3:2: "That ye may be mindful of the words which were spoken before by the holy Prophets and of the commandment of us, the Apostles of the Lord and Savior." In addition there must be cited the passage which was referred to once before, 2 Pet. 3:16: "As also in all his Epistles, speaking in them of these things; in which are some things hard to be understood, which they that are unlearned and unstable wrest, as they do also the other Scriptures, unto their own destruction." Let the reader here note the words "the *other* Scriptures." Paul's Epistles are spoken of, and St. Peter evidently assigns them the rank of Scripture; for in speaking of the rest of the Bible, he uses the term "the *other* Scriptures." It is clear, then, that if we regard the writings of the Apostles in the light of New Testament teaching, they must be viewed as being of divine origin, having been produced by the Holy Spirit.

INSPIRATION NOT MECHANICAL

A few general remarks need to be appended here. While the Bible clearly indicates, with respect to the origin of the Scriptures, that God employed human beings to do the work of writing (cf. Matt. 1:22: "Now, all this was done that it might be fulfilled which was spoken of the Lord by the Prophet"), there is nothing in the statements of Scripture on this subject to make us assume that the holy writers were mere machines, who in a mechanical manner were jotting down what was being dictated to them. On the contrary, the evidence we have makes such a view impossible. To point to but one circumstance, the Epistles of Paul, while truly inspired, are evidently not merely something he passed on to others as secretary, but they are the outflowings of the great heart of this remarkable servant of God. Cf. Rom. 15:15: "Nevertheless, brethren, I have written the more boldly unto you in some sort, as putting you in mind, because of the grace that is given to me of God." Gal. 4:19, 20: "My little children, of whom I travail in birth again until Christ be formed in you, I desire to be present with you now and to change my voice; for I stand in doubt of you." Gal. 6:11: "Ye see how large a letter I have written unto you with mine own hand." To assume that Paul was acting solely in the role of a dictograph would be giving the lie to his explicit statements.

Furthermore, the Scripture passages adduced teach that not only parts of the Bible, but all of it, and not merely its thoughts, but its very words have come from God. The Scripture as we have it before us is declared to be God-breathed, and we know it consists of sentences and words. "It is written," says the Savior, appealing to the exact words as recorded in the Bible. Paul likewise in Gal. 3:16, when referring to the Old Testament prophecy, stresses the fact that the singular is used and not the plural, saying: "Now, to Abraham and his Seed were the promises made. He saith not, And to seeds, as of many, but as of one, And to thy Seed, which is Christ." Evidently in his view every word of the Scriptures is God-given. We therefore have to reject the view which has been circulated during the last years with a great deal of zeal, that the ideas, the doctrines, of the Bible, may be considered as divine, but not the very words.

Proof of the Bible's Truthfulness

In the above we glanced at what the Bible says about itself — the Scripture doctrine of inspiration. This doctrine we accept as true. The testimony of the Bible as to its origin and character is the chief factor inducing us to believe it to be inspired. The objection which is hurled against this position, that it will not do to prove the Bible's inspiration by an appeal to what it says about itself (proving inspiration by assuming inspiration, as it is called); that, when a stranger comes to us, we are not satisfied to have him establish his identity by what he asserts about himself; that identification has to be made by a reliable third party, does not cause Bible Christians a minute's difficulty. The truth is that the Bible has proved its worth and reliability to them; for that reason they can accept its statements without hesitation. You may be skeptical when strangers approach you using very complimentary language about themselves. But if a stranger befriends you before you can befriend him, if he shows himself a trustworthy, reliable person, you do not reject his statements when he gives an account of himself.

Think of how the Bible has given evidence of its truthfulness and credibility! It has told us of our sins, holding up to our view as in a mirror the condition of our heart. It has told us of the judgments of God which we have deserved, and our conscience has confirmed the dread sentence of condemnation. Next it has told us of the help which the love of God has prepared for us poor sinners, speaking in such a convincing, winning way that our hearts were melted and we joyfully accepted the message of God's mercy, finding there the peace and rest which we elsewhere had sought in vain. Moreover, by its proclamation of reconciliation and pardon it influences our lives so that we become different people, new creatures, serving God and our neighbor with a glad heart, anxious to please our Father in heaven. Thus it has proved that it is a divine force. You will not mistrust the stranger, will you, who assists you in many ways, who risks his own life to save yours when you are in danger and leads you to realize visions of happiness you had long entertained in vain? Ah, he ceases to be a stranger and becomes your friend, and you would spurn the thought of requesting him to identify himself by the witness of a third party. There you have the case of the Bible as Bible Christians view it. The truthfulness of the Book is apparent. Why should we believe everything else it says, but hesitate to accept what it tells us about its origin?

INFALLIBILITY OF THE BIBLE

A corollary of the doctrine of the inspiration of the Bible is the teaching that it is infallible. When on the following pages we study paragraphs of the Scriptures on which Bible critics or our own hearts have cast suspicion as to their correctness or their agreement with divine truth, we shall set about our investigation with the conviction that not the Bible is at fault, but its critics, whoever they may be. The justice of the charge that this is too sweeping an assumption, that it is unscientific, because no investigator, if he is of the right sort, will determine beforehand what the nature of his findings will be, positive or negative, in keeping with former theories, or opposed to them — I say the justice of this charge we cannot allow. If the Bible comes from God in every part, it is infallible. God — of that we are sure — will neither err nor willfully deceive us. If he did either, He would not be God, the holy, the omniscient Creator. Since the divine authorship of the Bible is settled for us, its infallibility follows as a matter of course. Besides, there are clear Scripture declarations teaching the infallibility of the Bible. Ps. 119 has some specific statements to this effect. V. 160 we read: "Thy Word is true from the beginning; and every one of Thy righteous judgments endureth forever," and v. 140 exalts the Scriptures thus: "Thy Word is very pure; therefore Thy servant loveth it." To New Testament writings the words of St. Paul apply, 2 Thess. 2:15: "Therefore, brethren, stand fast, and hold the traditions which ye have been taught, whether by word or our Epistle." These passages imply that the writings of the Apostles and Prophets, as they left the hands of their inspired authors, were without error.

THE BIBLE'S CHIEF THEME IS CHRIST
AND HIS SALVATION

One great danger for people who engage in studies like the one we are starting on is that the Bible for them gets to be a book of puzzles and problems, which they attack with a lively intellect, but which engage their attention and industry to such an extent that they have no time for anything else in the Scriptures and are reading them solely with an eye to difficulties on which they may exercise their ingenuity. It is very regrettable if anyone uses the Book of Life in such a fashion. The same thing is true of the person who reads the Bible merely on account of the exalted poetry it contains or the pure, forceful English of the King James Version and of the man who wishes to use it simply as a source book in his historical and archaeological researches and of the pupils who have been told that in the Bible we have some of the best short stories that were ever written and who are paging through the sacred volume in quest of such pieces of literature. These people are right in a measure — the Bible does offer what they are looking for; and still they are wrong, because, in searching for pearls, they fail to lay hold of the one truly precious pearl, the pardon of God provided by the sacrifice of Jesus Christ. These folk are as foolish as the prisoner who is sent a letter of pardon by the governor and who admires the envelope, the seal, the beautiful script of the governor's note, but fails to acquaint himself with its contents.

What the Scriptures are intended for is beautifully stated by St. Paul in 2 Tim. 3:15, 16: "And that from a child thou hast known the Holy Scriptures, which are able to make thee wise unto salvation through faith which is in Christ Jesus. All Scripture is given by inspiration of God and is profitable for doctrine, for reproof, for correction, for instruction in righteousness, that the man of God may be perfect, throughly furnished unto all good works." To bring us to faith in Christ Jesus, to teach us divine, heavenly truths, to correct us when we fall into error or sinful ways of living, to inform us as to the works which our God delights in, and finally to lead us to heaven, that is the real purpose of the Bible. Its aims are spiritual. In dealing with some difficulties, it will be helpful if we bear this in mind. When we now and then find information on historical matters to be rather meager, when our native curiosity is not satisfied with what is offered, when scientific data which men are anxious to possess are not furnished, when events which we should like to see suppressed are spread on the open page with many a detail while others whose description we should enjoy are dismissed in a few words, then let us ask ourselves whether the reason for what we count a disappointing feature does not lie in the special purpose of the Bible, to lead us to salvation by faith in Christ Jesus.

THE BIBLE IS A CLEAR BOOK

In giving consideration to the passages of the Scriptures that have been called difficult, we must likewise adhere to the fundamental principle that the Bible is a clear book, all the talk of obscure sections and the great number of commentaries notwithstanding. Little details may have some darkness hovering over them, but the great themes of the Scriptures, which can be put into two words, Sin and Grace, or Law and Gospel, are treated with magnificent perspicuity on almost every page, and he who has his heart's chords attuned to these central notes finds the lessons of the Scripture very intelligible. Again, I am well aware that one class of people will call the Bible a hopelessly obscure volume, namely, all those who wish to understand what finite minds simply cannot grasp, the nature of God, the creation of the world out of nothing, the mysteries connected with Christ's person and work, the resurrection of all bodies at the end of the world, and similar things. Those who approach it expecting to find information showing them, for instance, by means of what chemical process the omnipotence of Jesus changed water into wine, will be sadly disappointed. God and His works are spoken of; they are not explained in scientific formulae.

This makes many sections of the Bible unacceptable to those haughty minds whose motto is to reject as untrue whatever they cannot comprehend. The simple Bible Christian, however, who trusts in God's power and truthfulness, will not experience much difficulty when he reads the Scriptures. He cannot demonstrate the truth of its statements on supernatural things by the methods of laboratories, but what the statements signify is perfectly patent to him. To give an example, he knows of no reason why he should call the account of how Jesus raised Lazarus after the latter had been dead several days an obscure passage. It is very true that he cannot show scientifically how Jesus performed this miracle (except by pointing to the deity of our Lord), but the narrative of this great miracle has nothing in it which he could call obscure. When we place ourselves into this attitude, we can understand the Scripture passages in which the Bible is called clear and a light, for example, Ps. 119:105: "Thy Word is a lamp unto my feet and a light unto my path"; and v. 130: "The entrance of Thy words giveth light; it giveth understanding unto the simple"; and 2 Pet. 1:19: "We have also a more sure Word of Prophecy, whereunto ye do well that ye take heed, as unto a light that shineth in a dark place, until the day dawn, and the Daystar arise in your hearts."

SOME FURTHER PRINCIPLES THAT ARE TO BE OBSERVED IN DEALING WITH DIFFICULT PASSAGES IN THE SCRIPTURES

After pondering what view we have to take of the Bible, the reader may welcome a brief discussion of some other important general considerations which he ought to bear in mind when confronted by Scripture passages which appear difficult to him. The following discussion is not intended to be exhaustive; but I hope that one or the other of my readers will be benefited by what will here be submitted.

1. By all means, when we have come upon a Scripture passage which is causing us trouble, let us look at it prayerfully. What will a pious, obedient, loving child do when it hears the father make a remark which on the face of it appears objectionable? Instead of criticizing him and condemning his utterance as wrong, the child will ask him for an explanation. If we find stumbling blocks in the Holy Scriptures, let us take the attitude of such a loving child. It is safe to say that very many obstacles

will be removed at once when God is implored for light and help. The grand promise: "Ask, and it shall be given you; seek, and ye shall find; knock, and it shall be opened unto you," will be fulfilled. If we continue in such prayers year after year, the pages of the sacred Book will all the time become more luminous to us. Every one of us who is much beset by doubts on account of difficulties which he thinks he finds in the Scriptures has every reason to ask himself whether he prays frequently and persistently enough in studying them.

2. Hand in hand with the spirit of prayer must and will be found the spirit of humility. Whoever approaches the Bible in haughtiness, thinking that his intellectual powers are quite sufficient for the solution of all difficulties, will either have to change his attitude, or he will soon flounder in the mire of unbelief. We should never forget the prayer which Jesus uttered, recorded Matt. 11:25, 26: "I thank Thee, O Father, Lord of heaven and earth, because Thou hast hid these things from the wise and prudent and hast revealed them unto babes. Even so, Father; for so it seemed good in Thy sight." The mysteries of God's revelation require humble hearts to be received. The proud and the haughty will turn away from the rich banquet table of God's holy Word in supercilious scorn without satisfying their hunger, while the meek and lowly here find manna for their famished souls.

3. Another important advice to give to all who speak of difficulties in the Scriptures is that they must not be satisfied with reading the passages in question once or twice, but must reread them again and again. Experience

has shown that persistency in the study of difficult portions of the Scriptures will frequently yield surprisingly gratifying results. "Search the Scriptures," John 5:39, has its application here, too.

SCRIPTURE MUST INTERPRET ITSELF

4. Among the principles of Bible interpretation one of the most prominent is that we must let Scripture explain Scripture, or, to put it differently, we must let the Bible interpret itself. Where this principle is adhered to, not only will mistakes be avoided which are very commonly made, but difficulties will be overcome which can be solved in no other way. To give an example, we are all familiar with the cry of woe our divine Savior uttered on the cross, "My God, My God, why hast Thou forsaken Me?" It is a cry which is reported in Matt. 27:46 and Mark 15:34. More than one of us, I am sure, have marveled why Matthew and Mark, after reporting this cry, tell us that at once after its utterance one of the bystanders took a sponge and filled it with vinegar and put it on a reed and gave Jesus to drink. The matter is fully explained in the Gospel according to St. John, where we are told that Jesus uttered another cry: "I thirst," which induced a bystander to take the action reported.

To give another example or two: Many a Bible reader has been perplexed when he reads, Heb. 12:17, about Esau: "For ye know how that afterward, when he would have inherited the blessing, he was rejected; for he found no place for repentance, though he sought it carefully with tears." The reader might think that the Holy Book here states Esau was not permitted to repent even though he wished to become a different person. But let us compare Scripture with Scripture, turning to Gen. 27:34 ff., where the story of Esau is first told, and we shall find our difficulty removed. The latter passage shows that the repentance which Esau was seeking with tears was a change of mind in his father, whom he sought to persuade to bless him also. The Greek word for repentance, it is important to remember, literally means "change of mind." What Esau was denied, then, was not permission personally to undergo a change of heart, but to induce his father to alter his decision.

When a Christian reads the regulations concerning sacrifices in the ritual of the Old Testament Tabernacle and Temple, he often wonders why there was all this slaughtering of animals and what purpose God had in view when He ordered these bloody ceremonies. This is a big subject, far too many-sided and profound for a little paragraph, but the point to be emphasized here is that the patient Bible reader will find light in the Holy Book itself on this question. In the Epistle to the Hebrews, chap. 10:1, he will read this sentence: "For the Law, having a shadow of good things to come and not the very image of the things, can never with those sacrifices which they offered year by year continually make the comers thereunto perfect." The Law had a shadow of good things to come, the holy writers say. These are the words which I here should like to emphasize, because they throw light on the Old Testament ceremonies, which we too often are apt to find meaningless. The sacrifices, as the statement declares, could not make those perfect that offered them; but they were a shadow of good things to come, they pointed forward and thus were prophetic, directing the gaze of the worshiper to that one great sacrifice which was to make full atonement for all sins. In this manner Scripture interprets Scripture.

5. Again, it is necessary to remember that in reading the English Bible we are dealing with a translation. While our King James Version is a good translation, there is always the possibility that a certain difficult verse or word has not been rendered adequately. Now and then a reference to the original Hebrew or Greek will quickly clear up a difficulty which confronts us. The following words of F. E. Gaebelein (*Exploring the Bible,* p. 187) are to the point: "The Bible was written originally in Hebrew and in Greek. The Authorized, or King James, Version, our finest translation from a literary point of view, was made more than three hundred years ago. Since then new and valuable ancient manuscripts of both Old and New Testaments have been discovered. Textual criticism has been developed to a high degree of efficiency. As a result many inaccuracies of rendering have been corrected. With the various revised versions at hand, with an analytical concordance, with reliable commentaries, and with the help of dictionaries of the Bible language, the reader need not know Greek or Hebrew to verify the original meaning of a given passage. He has in his mother tongue the means whereby he may determine the correctness of most of the obscure translations." To give an instance showing how recourse to the original may aid us in understanding a Scripture passage, I shall mention Phil. 3:20, where our Authorized Version

reads: "For our *conversation* is in heaven." This is an utterly obscure statement to most readers. Even those who recall that formerly the English word conversation was used in the sense of conduct will find Paul's words hardly intelligible. The fog disappears at once, however, when the Greek New Testament is consulted, where the words in question, translated literally, read: "Our *citizenship* is in heaven." What a flood of light does this not throw on the passage, and what a beautiful and important message rings out from it when thus rendered! Living here on earth, we are in reality citizens of heaven; our true home is above.

INTERPRETATION OF FIGURATIVE LANGUAGE

6. Furthermore, we must not overlook that certain passages or sections in the Scriptures are written in figurative language. Every Bible reader will at once think of the Book of Revelation, which is full of striking symbols and figures. All will agree that figurative language must not be treated as if the statements were to be taken literally. To do so would be tantamount to doing violence to the meaning of the author. When a writer uses metaphors, he means his readers to understand him metaphorically. When, for instance, the Scriptures speak of the "right arm" of God, we must not interpret the expression to signify that our great God has a human body. In this case we are dealing with a figure of speech which has reference merely to the power of God. It is a metaphor which we still employ. Thus when we say that the strong hand of a certain political dictator crushes all opposition, no one will give to this statement a literal

meaning. The reverse of the principle just enunciated is, of course, true also, namely, that an expression which is devoid of figurative features must not be interpreted symbolically. The dividing line between these two species of language is not always easily drawn. Here, too, the prayerful and humble Bible reader will progress in insight and knowledge.

7. Another major principle of Scripture interpretation is that we must interpret passages that are obscure and figurative by those that are clear and contain no metaphors. No matter who the author is with whom we are dealing, it is but fair that we interpret his less intelligible utterances in the light of those which are perfectly clear. The unity of the Scriptures, the fact that one Author is speaking in all the books, from Genesis to Revelation, compels us to apply this principle in interpreting any part of the Bible. It follows that, since the New Testament is more clear than the Old, we must interpret the writings of the Old Covenant by those of the New. If we proceeded in the vice-versa fashion, we should be unfair to our Holy Book.

THE CONTEXT

8. Again, let us remember when studying a passage that the context in which it is found must be carefully scrutinized. Gaebelein says very correctly (*op. cit.*, page 182): "Isolated passages are generally misleading if considered apart from their context. Mere common sense supports the truth of this view. Every prominent public speaker suffers from this abuse by the newspapers. How often a totally false impression of a sermon or an address has resulted from publicity wrongly given to some

single striking statement!" How unfair, for instance, to consider the words of Jesus, Luke 10:28: "This do, and thou shalt live," apart from their context and to construe them to say that Jesus taught work-righteousness. Looking at the connection in which these words were spoken, we see that He addresses them to a self-righteous lawyer who has just quoted the two chief commandments of the Law and to whom Jesus wishes to bring home the insufficiency and weakness of all his efforts. In the same way the words of Jesus spoken of the woman who had been a sinner, Luke 7:47: "Her sins, which are many, are forgiven, for she loved much," might be interpreted to mean that love procures forgiveness, while a study of the context, especially of the parable of Jesus spoken on this occasion, vv. 40-43, shows that love here is referred to as the result of the forgiveness, much grace and mercy producing much love.

9. Finally, the historical circumstances involved must be given consideration in studying a difficult passage. Often careful scrutiny of the time in which an author lived and the circumstances under which he wrote will shed light on the meaning of statements which at first appear puzzling to us. For instance, when St. John in 1 John 4:3 says: "Every spirit that confesseth not that Jesus Christ is come in the flesh is not of God," we are surprised at the description which is given us of spirits that are antichristian. Why are they characterized as spirits that confess not that Jesus Christ is come in the flesh? The whole matter becomes very clear to us when we learn that John is opposing false teachers who taught the wicked doctrine that the Jesus who had lived on

earth was not the Christ, the Messiah, and that the Messiah had not in Him assumed human form. It is in antithesis to these heretics that St. John writes, for instance, John 1:14: "The Word was made flesh and dwelt among us," etc. Many similar instances could be adduced.

If the above brief directions, the list of which is not meant to be exhaustive, are followed, I can confidently predict that most of the difficulties which people find in reading the Scriptures will disappear, and the old Book will appear more lovely and full of helpful meaning than ever.

Having defined the attitude in which we shall approach the Scriptures as a whole, we shall now look at the most outstanding passages labeled difficult, it being my hope that the reader, by being shown how some of these difficulties can be overcome, will be enabled himself to solve others which are not specifically treated in this little volume.

On the question whether the Gospel story is reliable the book of Dr. Ad. Haentzschel, *The Great Quest* (Concordia Publishing House, 1953), can be read with much profit. Cf. especially chap. 10 (p. 105ff.).

PART TWO

The Miracles of the Bible

NATURE OF MIRACLES

One criticism of our sacred Book which is frequently heard is that it relates things which are improbable or downright impossible; in other words, that it reports miracles as historical facts. The accounts under consideration are not attacked as obscure, but as untrue. Here we evidently have a large class of passages causing difficulty to some people, and we have to look a little more closely at them. A miracle is an act which transcends human powers of accomplishment and human ability of explanation. It is not an unnatural occurrence, but a supernatural one. At times it may be exactly like a natural event; but the conditions under which it takes place are such that we classify it as a miracle, for instance, when rain comes in answer to prayer, as in the case of Elijah, 1 Kings 18:41 ff.; James 5:17 f.

When a miracle takes place, God Himself intervenes and makes His presence felt in a special manner. Egypt was visited by a destructive hailstorm when Pharaoh refused to let the children of Israel depart in obedience to the command of God, Ex. 9:22 ff. Now, though hailstorms are regarded as perfectly natural occurrences, still this particular one constituted a miracle because of

25

its extraordinary vehemence and because it was sent by God as a special sign and as a punishment for the wickedness of the Egyptian king. The Bible is full of reports of miraculous happenings. The chain of such events begins on the first page, in the story of the creation of the world, and it continues to the last page, where the message of an angel who brought revelations to John is recorded, Rev. 22:8. These miracles are of many different kinds, some occurring in inanimate nature, others, on and in man; some visible, others invisible; some bringing health, others bringing punishment; some performed without human agents, others, through Prophets, Apostles, etc. If we take everything miraculous out of the Bible, how little will there be left!

WHY ARE THE ACCOUNTS OF MIRACLES REJECTED BY SOME PEOPLE?

As intimated before, it is just this miraculous element in the Scriptures which is the chief stumbling block for many people when they are asked to submit to the guidance of the Bible. The notorious unbelievers and agnostics who made a name for themselves by publicly and loudly opposing the divine character of the Scriptures, for instance, Tom Paine, Voltaire, and Ingersoll, were in arms especially against the accounts of miracles in our Holy Book. The attitude of such people is that miracles are impossible and that hence all these narratives of supernatural occurrences must be untrue. Miracles are not happening nowadays, they did not happen in ancient times either — so runs the argument. What shall we say?

If a person does not believe in a personal God who has

made and who governs the universe, heaven and earth and all they contain, it is natural for him to reject the Scripture accounts of miracles. The atheist is consistent when he refuses to believe they can occur. But I hope that no reader of this book will adopt the view of the fool who says in his heart: "There is no God," Ps. 14:1. If we are thrown into contact with such people, it is of no use that we argue with them about the credibility of the Scriptures. There is something still more fundamental on which agreement has to be reached before there can be profitable discussion, namely, the question of the existence of God. The Biblical narratives throughout presuppose the grand truth "that God *is* and that He is a rewarder of them that diligently seek Him," Heb. 11:6.

It cannot be denied, however, that there are many people who do not wish to be atheists, but who nevertheless doubt the possibility of miracles. God works according to certain laws, the laws of nature, they maintain, and nothing can happen that is contrary to these laws. This is an extraordinary position to assume, we reply. To believe in an almighty and omniscient God, on the one hand, and to deny, on the other, that He can set aside, suspend, or transcend the laws of nature is a deplorable inconsistency. Who is it that is God, the laws of nature or He who has made nature with its laws? Dr. L. Keyser very well says (*A System of Christian Evidence*, p. 58): "A God who would permit Himself to get caught in the machinery of His own make or who would voluntarily put Himself into it and never operate upon it from without, would, indeed, be a poor sort of a God."

TWO IMPORTANT CONSIDERATIONS
CONCERNING MIRACLES

Looking at the matter calmly, we have to say that it is an altogether unscientific position if anybody starts with the assumption that miracles cannot happen. How does he know? He is far from having that open mind which science says the investigator should have. The questions whether miracles do happen is entitled to the same fair treatment as other questions. Just as little as anybody will deny in advance, let us say, that a new comet has been discovered, so little let him make it the presupposition of his religious thinking that miracles are out of the question. The position of Voltaire, who is said to have declared that, even if a miracle were performed in the market place before his own eyes, he would not accept it, is grossly unscientific. The only question which is justified according to scientific procedure is whether there is any proof that the miracles related in the Scriptures actually occurred.

In a brilliant little book on radical Gospel criticism *(Darstellungen des Lebens Jesu)* Uhlhorn, a celebrated German theologian, looks at the question whether the position that the Bible miracles did not happen is tenable from the point of view of the scientific historian. For argument's sake he waives the inspiration of the Scriptures. One miracle the fair-minded critic will have to admit, he points out, and that is the greatest of them all, the resurrection of Christ. Even if you look upon the New Testament as nothing but a collection of ordinary human documents, you will have to grant this event occurred; the evidence for it is simply overwhelming. The same conclusion is reached, for instance, by the English author who, assuming the pen name Frank Morison, in 1930 published a book entitled *Who Moved the Stone?* What makes the verdict, after a searching, minute examination of all pertinent data, most impressive is the remarkable circumstance that he started out to prove the very opposite of what, as one aspect of the subject after the other was studied by him, he ultimately found to be true. The remarkable case of Lord Lyttleton and Mr. West, who set out to disprove, the former the miraculous element in the conversion of Paul, the latter the resurrection of Christ and who, when they met to compare notes, confessed that they had been conquered by the Bible, is another very heartening instance of this nature. It is not in keeping with the plan of this book to insert here a lengthy discussion on the evidence for the resurrection of our Savior. I must content myself with quoting a paragraph from Farrar's *Life of Christ,* chapter 62, in which he summarizes well the facts which even the unbeliever, if he is fair-minded, will have to grant: "That His body had not been removed by His enemies; that its absence caused to His disciples the profoundest amazement, not unmingled in the breasts of some of them with sorrow and alarm; that they subsequently became convinced, by repeated proofs, that He had indeed risen from the dead; that for the truth of this belief they were ready at all times themselves to die; that the belief effected a profound and total change in their character, making the timid courageous and the weak irresistible; that they were incapable of a conscious falsehood and that, even if it had not been so, a conscious falsehood could never have had power to convince the disbelief, and regenerate the morality, of the world; that on this belief of the resurrection were built the still universal observance of the first day of the week and the entire foundations of the Christian Church — these at any rate are facts which even skepticism itself, if it desires to be candid, can hardly fail, however reluctantly and slowly, to admit."

Firmly believing, then, that the merely historical evidence for the resurrection of Jesus is absolutely convincing, I say that here we have a miracle whose acceptance is not conditioned by belief in the infallibility of the Bible and whose actual occurrence cannot be successfully denied. But if this one miracle took place, then the possibility of the occurrence of miracles has to be granted, and the position of those people who deny that miracles ever happened becomes untenable.* Considerations like this should help persons who balk at Bible stories of miraculous events to overcome their prejudice and to listen to the message of the Scriptures.

MIRACLES AND OUR TIMES

Miracles do not happen nowadays, we are told. Why should we assume that they did occur in days of old? I reply, Is it really true that there are no longer any miraculous events? There are but few believers in the

---

* See Gore, *Can We Then Believe?* pp. 52, 53: "So again Professor Hobson asserts that science properly so called can meet the claims of miracles with no a priori negative. And Dr. Tennant, in his admirable little book *Miracle and Its Philosophical Presuppositions,* has provided what I should venture to call a demonstration that miracles cannot on scientific or philosophical grounds be ruled out as impossible. It is a question of history."

Savior who cannot point to an occasion where God heard their prayer when the outlook was desperate and He furnished them the help they needed. Every experience of this kind brings us proof that God is a doer of miracles. I shall grant, of course, that, as far as our observation is able to judge, the Lord is not performing miracles today in the striking, overawing manner which He employed 1900 years ago. Why He permits such a difference to arise and to exist, why it is that, as we view the world's history, we notice an ebb and flow of miraculous happenings, years of plenty being followed by years of drought, He has not revealed to us.

An explanation which has frequently been advanced with respect to the absence of signs and wonders in our own day, and which does not seem farfetched, is that miracles no longer are needed as they were in the days when the Church was founded. At that time, when skepticism and unbelief were encountered by the disciples of Jesus on all sides and the question was heard, How will these people prove that the new message they proclaim is true? it was of utmost importance that confirmation should come to their proclamation by special acts of God. Now that the Church is established, it is sufficient that its message be proved true by the influence of the Holy Spirit in the lives of Christians. The absence of spectacular signs and wonders in our days therefore can well be accounted for and need not disturb anybody.

CLEARNESS OF THE ACCOUNTS

In proceeding to view a little more particularly some Biblical accounts of miracles, we shall soon perceive that these narratives do not need many comments, as though they were unclear. Wonderful, awe-inspiring, they are, but not obscure, as a rule.

The story of the collapse of the walls about Jericho can be understood by every reader of ordinary intelligence; no commentary is required to elucidate its language. How God did it, what unseen forces He summoned to hurl the proud battlements to the ground, whether He perhaps sent an ordinary earthquake, which rocked the region so violently that the walls were rent and thrown down, is something we cannot tell because the inspired narrative is silent on this point. But what I wish to stress here is, not the *account* is obscure and unintelligible, but the manner in which the event took place. If you believe that God is omnipotent and that He in mysterious ways can and will intervene to help His children, then these reports of miracles will present no difficulty to you.

NO FREAK MIRACLES

Another feature worthy of remark is that many of the miracles follow what we term natural law, though at the same time transcending it. When Jesus feeds the five thousand, Matt. 14:14 ff., how does He do it? He might have removed their hunger with a word; for with God nothing is impossible. But instead of employing such a method, He provides bread to feed the people, satisfying their hunger and sustaining their lives by the usual means. When the children of Israel were pursued by Pharaoh and, it seemed, would not be able to escape, the Red Sea forming what appeared to be an insuperable barrier to further flight, God prepared a way for them, so that they could cross to the other side without difficulty. It is clear that by the exercise of His omnipotence He might have saved them from Pharaoh's grasp in a different way. For instance, He could have transported the whole host through the air to a region of safety. Instead of this, Israel has to march just as it marched before.

The lesson which this suggests is an important one. God does not perform freak miracles. He helps His children through His power, but, as a rule, it is by using the very channels along which His gifts ordinarily come to them. A certain country is visited by a disastrous drought and the resulting famine. Relief comes from God, not in the form of gold falling down from heaven, but in the shape of rain and a few years of plenty. The tuberculosis patient prays to God for help in what appears to be a case of fatal illness. God preserves his life, however, not by one majestic command, but through making it possible for him to remove to a salubrious climate, where sunshine and pure air restore his health. The plagues in Egypt are very instructive if viewed in this light. Cf. Ex. 7—12. In almost every instance they consisted of a visitation which might arise in the ordinary course of events, and still a miraculous element attached to each one, manifesting itself in the time when the plague occurred and in its peculiar virulence.

JESUS NOT PERFORMING MIRACLES IN NAZARETH

A passage which requires some comment here is Mark 6:5, 6, referring to the visit of Jesus in Nazareth. We are told there: "He could there do no mighty work save that

He laid His hands upon a few sick folk and healed them. And He marveled because of their unbelief." Does this deny that Jesus is omnipotent and the true God? Nothing of the sort. It simply points out that, if the gifts of God are to be received, there must be a receptive attitude on the part of man, that our Lord will not force His beneficent ministrations on anybody, that those who persistently refuse to accept what He offers will not receive it. It is very true that this receptive attitude itself is a gift of God. But what we are concerned with here is the truth that God's wonderful works are not performed for those who spurn them. Is it not here perhaps that we have a partial explanation for the absence of striking miracles, universally recognized as such, in our own day? The generation is an unbelieving one, calling itself enlightened, puffed up with a sense of its own wisdom and importance. It ridicules the idea of miracles; hence it has to remain without events which it would classify as such.

THE HEALING OF A BOY WHO WAS
A DEMONIAC

There will probably occur to the reader what is recorded Mark 9:29: "And He [Jesus] said unto them, This kind can come forth by nothing but by prayer and fasting." The disciples of Jesus are addressed. On their journey through Galilee they had performed miracles of healing, and they had expelled demons. In the case of which we read Mark 9:14 ff. they had not been able to bring about the expulsion. Jesus chides them for their unbelief, but says in conclusion: "This kind can come forth by nothing but by prayer and fasting." Was there, then, something more than faith required on this occasion? Must the saying of Jesus in which He depicts the power of faith as sufficiently great to move mountains be modified and held not to pertain to the healing of certain cases of demoniac possession? Such is not the meaning of Jesus. The fact of which He wishes to remind His disciples is that an affliction like that of the poor boy they had been dealing with was so dreadful, so terrifying, in its nature that strong faith was needed if they contemplated giving help to such an unfortunate being and that their faith had to be strengthened through earnest prayer, aided by fasting, before entering upon this battle with Satan.

MIRACLES IN THE EARLY CHURCH

In the early Church many of the believers were endowed with miraculous powers, as is evident, for instance, from 1 Cor. 12 and 14. Let the reader peruse these chapters, especially 1 Cor. 12:8-10. A few words on the spiritual gifts mentioned there will not be amiss. It will be noticed that some of the endowments which Paul mentions must at once be classified as supernatural, while others are found with Christians today and would not be given that attribute. But the Apostle calls them all gifts of the Spirit — a hint to us not to say that the Holy Spirit no longer is operating. Some of the Corinthian Christians were given the word of wisdom. Their endowment, it seems, consisted in the ability to give wise counsel resting on the Word of God. Others, again, had been given the word of knowledge, that is, the faculty to discern the deep things in the Scriptures and to give fitting utterance to their thoughts on these lofty themes. Some had received "faith," which I take to mean a special or extraordinary measure or degree of faith, strong to withstand vehement attacks. Others had been endowed with the gift of healing, with the ability to perform miraculous cures.

Then there was a group which had been given the ability to work miracles in general, that is, to do mighty, supernatural things. Some had the gift of prophecy. To them the Holy Spirit granted special revelations, which they proclaimed and applied with penetrating, gripping power; at times they also foretold future events. Others were able to discern spirits, that is, to tell whether teachers whom they came in contact with were sent by God or whether they came of their own accord. Perhaps the most extraordinary gift in our view was that designated "divers kinds of tongues," which, as far as we are able to establish, consisted in a sort of ecstatic speech, which no one could understand unless one possessed the gift of interpretation of tongues; and there were people on whom this latter faculty had been bestowed. The above shows that it was a marvelously endowed congregation which Paul had founded at Corinth, and we need not assume that he presents an exhaustive list of the gifts with which its members were adorned. In other congregations there may have been similar manifestations of supernatural endowments. Bearing this in mind, we can more easily understand why the early Church grew by leaps and bounds in spite of violent opposition from Jews and Gentiles.

DO MEN WORK MIRACLES TODAY?

In this connection a passage may be examined which is here and there perplexing people, Mark 16:17 f. Cf. also Luke 10:19. Jesus here gives the definite promise that miraculous powers will attend those that believe. Must it not, then, be conceded that certain radical sects which appeal to miraculous healings in proof of their possession of the truth are standing on solid Scriptural ground? My reply is: Let us not violate the majesty of the Word of God by putting a question mark alongside the promises of the Savior. He bestows grand powers on believers, that is certain. But another matter which is very clear, too, is that, if anybody arises claiming the possession of miraculous gifts, but contradicting the revealed Word of God in any point, he is not to be followed by us. Such powers as he possesses or pretends to possess, if used to propagate error, are not from God, but from the Prince of Darkness.

In the Old Testament God warns the children of Israel not to follow a prophet who will teach them to believe in other gods, in spite of signs and wonders which he may perform. Deut. 13:1-3 God tells them: "If there arise among you a prophet or a dreamer of dreams and giveth thee a sign or wonder and the sign or the wonder come to pass whereof he spake unto thee, saying, Let us go after other gods which thou hast not known and let us serve them, thou shalt not hearken unto the words of that prophet or that dreamer of dreams; for the Lord, your God, proveth you to know whether ye love the Lord, your God, with all your heart and with all your soul." And in the New Testament a similar note is sounded when St. Paul, 2 Thess. 2:9, depicts the Antichrist as appearing "after the working of Satan, with all power and signs and lying wonders." Miracles, taken by themselves, are not an absolute touchstone of the genuineness of the claims a teacher, or preacher, may put forth. The Church is built on the foundation of the Apostles and Prophets, Eph. 2:20, and if anybody lays a different foundation, he is not to be listened to, may his signs be ever so spectacular and numerous.

Another important point to remember in this connection is that miracles are granted by God and must not be "attempted." To try to perform them without having the assurance that God wants us to engage in them would be tempting the Lord, which in every case is a very reprehensible act. Cf. Matt. 4:7. The Apostles, when sent out on their first mission journey, performed miracles as a matter of course. You have the explanation in Matt. 10:8 and the parallel passages, where we are told that Jesus bestowed this faculty on them and ordered them to do such works.

The miracles, it must finally not be overlooked, were to *follow* those that believe, Mark 16:17. The context shows the preaching of the Gospel is most important, not miracles. If anybody makes them the chief factor in his ministry, giving them precedence to everything else, we can be sure that his work is not in keeping with the will of God. How little did the Apostles, when they preached the Word in the various parts of the world, put their miraculous gifts into the foreground! Arriving in a certain town, they did not gather the people to stage some wonderful performance before them; but they preached the good news of the kingdom of God established by the work and sacrifice of our Lord Jesus Christ. In the course of their stay in that town, if occasion arose, miracles might be performed, testifying that this new message was indeed the power of God unto salvation to every one that believes. But there was no thought of making a display of supernatural powers merely to attract the curious or to entertain the multitudes.

THE CURSING OF THE FIG TREE

A remark or two about the miracle of Jesus when He cursed the fig tree and made it wither may find a place in this chapter. Cf. Matt. 21:17. It is a miracle on which unbelieving critics have pounced, declaring that it was unworthy of our Lord. One of them blasphemously remarks that Jesus, "out of humor after the controversy with His enemies, finds a target for His wrath in an innocent tree which bare naught but leaves and flowers at this season." For the greater part the miracles of Jesus were acts of healing, helping people in their distress, and bringing joy to oppressed hearts. When He worked wonders in the sphere of external nature, when He, for instance, stilled the storm on the sea, it was for the purpose of rendering aid to such as needed it.

The one seeming exception is the cursing of the fig tree. Bible Christians, however, have never experienced any difficulty when contemplating it, and a little reflection will show them what answer to make to the wicked accuser of our Lord. In the first place, this miracle did not cause any pain or suffering. Furthermore, it showed the Apostles the omnipotence of their Master and furnished Him an opportunity to instruct them on the power of faith. Again, some Bible students have conjectured quite plausibly that Jesus here wished to furnish His disciples in a symbolical way a description of the Jewish nation, devoid of God-pleasing fruit, as it was, and of its terrible punishment. I might add that the leafy appearance of the tree gave a traveler the right to look for figs on it, because, as Edersheim remarks: "It is a well-known fact that in Palestine the fruit [of the fig tree] appears before the leaves." Since leaves were there, it was fair to assume that fruit was there, too. Considering all these matters, the shocking injustice of the blasphemers who dare to criticize our Lord's conduct in this episode becomes apparent to us.

DESTRUCTIVE MIRACLES

But what, it may be asked, of the miracles that were done for the very purpose of destroying men's lives, bringing grief and woe to many households? Such an act was performed when Elijah twice let fire fall from heaven and each time fifty-one men were consumed, 2 Kings 1:9 ff. We may here think, too, of the death of Pharaoh and his host in the sea when they were pursuing the Israelites, Ex. 14:26 ff. A brief word or two will here be sufficient. When the soldiers in the instance referred to were killed, God meted out punishment to the wicked rulers whom they served. Whether all, or at least most of them, were themselves ungodly, we do not know, neither need we assume that they were. Many a good Christian soldier who not through his own choice was fighting for an unrighteous cause perished on the field of battle; his body suffered, but his soul was saved. He fell because his wicked ruler or general was to be punished.

Furthermore, in the case of the two captains, just as well as in that of Pharaoh, God showed that He will not be mocked. If people think they can oppose the Almighty and openly defy Him, His wrath may quickly manifest itself in their destruction. And finally, the rebuke of Jesus administered to James and John when they, after the manner of Elijah, wished to call down fire upon the Samaritan village which had refused to give lodging to the little band, Luke 9:52 ff., must not be looked upon as implying a criticism of the action of Elijah. The two cases were entirely different. To mention but one point, for Elijah the fire furnished protection from persecution; James and John, however, wish to avenge an insult offered their Master and themselves. The rebuke of Jesus indicates that they were not actuated by the right motives in their zeal. We have an illustration here of the famous saying: *Si duo idem faciunt, non est idem* (if two do the same thing, it is not the same). What Elijah did was right. The same act, when attempted by the disciples of Jesus, was wrong, the situation being altogether different.

PART THREE

Moral Difficulties

AMONG the passages of the Scriptures which not only are seized upon with avidity by the enemies of the Christian faith, but somewhat perplex Christian Bible readers are those in which, seemingly, acts are ascribed to God or to men of God which our moral sense, our conscience, balks at, refusing to sanction them as right and proper. The true child of God, feeling deeply his own sinfulness and being exceedingly grateful for the pardon offered him in the Gospel of Jesus Christ, will not be long disturbed by such passages, owing to his strong conviction that in the holy God, who has graciously condescended to accomplish his rescue, there can be no fault or blemish. The situation becomes somewhat different when he is confronted with attacks of unbelievers laying emphasis on such passages and requesting him to give an explanation. It is chiefly for instances of this kind that the present chapter is written.

THE BIBLE CHARGED WITH MORAL
IMPERFECTIONS

Lest the reader think that I am here speaking entirely of imaginary matters, I shall insert a quotation from a modernistic writer, Prof. W. M. Forrest, who in his book _Do Fundamentalists Play Fair?_ p. 76 f., writes thus: "Take the Fundamentalists first. They are committed to defending as a necessary part of Christianity everything that their infallible Bible attributes to God. To them it is impossible to hold that Old Testament ideas of God were often imperfect and erroneous. They can admit that anything about God not revealed in the Old Testament could be reserved for the New, that the old ideas were incomplete. But they cannot admit that conceptions of God in a barbarous age were false as set forth in Scripture. What the Old Testament said God was or did, and the motives and reasons He had for doing things, the Fundamentalist must accept as absolutely true. When God was angry with Israel and prompted David to make a census of the people so He would have an excuse for wreaking His wrath upon the king, He did so by destroying seventy thousand of the people. The account in Samuel says God tempted David to do it. That was before Jewish theology had invented the devil. As Isaiah puts it, God did everything, created darkness as well as light and did evil as well as good. When Chronicles was written centuries later, the inspired writer had no such notion of a verbally inerrant Bible as the Fundamentalists have. Hence he boldly changed the record and said Satan did the tempting. But in either case and in many others showing God cruel and vindictive we have a picture of God so alien to Christ's teaching that it is unfair to hold it as a part of Christian faith." This quotation suffices to show how in certain quarters our Holy Book and the great God whom it reveals are made sport of, as though they condoned, and at times even favored, immorality.

THIS POSITION EXAMINED

When looking at passages of this import, we must not only carefully examine the words of the texts in question, but the parallel accounts, too, if there are such, and in fact everything the Scriptures have to say on the subject involved. Surveying the whole body of Scripture teaching or narrative on a certain topic, we shall, as a rule, at once see that the objection of the enemies of the Bible becomes untenable from the point of view of the unbiased observer. Furthermore, when the accusation is directed against something that a man of God, for instance, a prophet, has done, we have to examine whether the respective action received divine sanction or not. Men of God were sinful beings in the past as well as they are such today. The mere fact that a certain deed of theirs is recorded in the Scriptures does not indicate that it received divine approval. And finally, if there should be an instance where, in spite of all our painstaking earnest researches, a difficulty remains, an instance where God does not justify His ways to man, let us not become blasphemers, but thank God for such light as He has given us and confidently expect the remaining darkness to be removed in the life to come, where we shall not see through a glass, darkly, and merely know in part, as is the case here, but see face to face and know even as we are known, 1 Cor. 13:9-12.

We shall now at once scrutinize the particular charges advanced by the critic quoted. Is there any proof that Old Testament ideas of God were imperfect and erroneous? One consideration at once annihilates this accusation, namely, the unqualified endorsement which

Jesus gives to the Old Testament. It will not do to say that the Old Testament teaches a different God from the New Testament; the evidence is mightily against such a view. Not with one syllable do Jesus and the Apostles repudiate the teaching of the Prophets concerning God. The two Testaments stand and fall together. When Jesus debates with the Sadducees about the resurrection of the dead, Matt. 22:29 ff., He says that God, speaking to Moses, calls Himself the God of Abraham, Isaac, and Jacob and that He is not the God of the dead, but of the living. It will be observed that He does not say the God of the Old Covenant calls Himself by such and such a name. For Him it is the true God that spoke to Moses at the burning bush. If, as it is charged, the ideas of the Old Testament concerning God at times are imperfect and erroneous, then Jesus' conception of God was imperfect and erroneous — a conclusion which is abhorrent to all true Christians and which apparently even the critic we are dealing with does not wish to draw.

Some Specific Passages

Again, we inquire, What conception of God does the critic have in mind when he ascribes false views of God to the Scripture of the Old Testament? Even a charitable judge will have to say that the paragraph quoted abounds more in downright abuse than in attempts at presenting real evidence. There are only two specific passages which he refers to, to fortify his charge, the first one being 2 Sam. 24:1, where we are told that God again was angry with Israel and moved David to number the people. What our critic wishes to say is that God in this Old Testament passage is pictured as "cruel and vindictive." The incident and passage referred to deserve special study. God's anger was again kindled against Israel, we are told. The particular sin or sins which caused God's wrath to be aroused are not mentioned. Perhaps it was the participation of a part of the people in the rebellion of Absalom and Sheba against their king which was the cause of the divine anger. We must remember that, as has well been said, this is a moral universe and wrongdoing brings down punishment on the guilty individual or nation.

If our critic cavils at the large number of Israelites who lost their lives in the ensuing plague (70,000), let him think of the millions that perished in the recent World War, which stupendous calamity Christians the world over view as a sign that God is angry with this sin-loving, vain, unbelieving generation. Is it right to call God "cruel" and "vindictive" when He metes out punishments, even on a large scale, to peoples that live in wickedness? Ought the critic not, rather than speculate about the justice of God's methods in governing the world, — a matter which is far too deep for us puny human beings to fathom, — consider what Jesus says, Luke 13:3: "Except ye repent, ye shall all likewise perish"? Our reply, then, is that, if the critic thinks the Old Testament narrative makes God out a cruel and vindictive ruler because He inflicts severe penalties for wrongdoing, he must hurl the same accusation at God today when he observes how the Lord governs the universe, unless he is willing to dethrone the Almighty and to allow Him no longer any share in the sending of plagues, famines, and other visitations.

We may here, in addition, advert to the allusion to a passage in Isaiah made by our critic in the paragraph quoted, where the Prophet is said to be ascribing everything to God, the creation of darkness as well as of light, the doing of evil as well as of good. The passage the critic has in mind is Is. 45:7, where God says: "I form the light and create darkness; I make peace and create evil; I, the Lord, do all these things." It is clear that God here claims absolute sovereignty for Himself. Is there anything in these words with which a Christian, standing on the New Testament, has to disagree? The universal reign of God is a subject which Jesus speaks of when He says that God makes His sun to rise on the evil and on the good and sends rain on the just and the unjust, Matt. 5:45; that He even clothes the grass of the field, Matt. 6:30. What causes some difficulty is the declaration that God creates evil. But the statement loses much of its difficulty when we take evil here in the sense of affliction, adverse occurrence, and not in the sense of sin, wrongdoing. Evidently, what the Lord is speaking of, according to the connection, contrasting light with darkness, peace with evil, is not moral, but physical evil, such as tempests, earthquakes, and similar calamities. It is true that our reason will continue to ask, How can the God who is said to be loving, inflict such harsh treatment on His creatures, subjecting them to suffering and manifold heartaches? A big chapter here presents itself for discussion. Some of the chief truths which here come before us are the following:

1. In governing the universe, God uses visitations in nature or calamities like war to punish the wicked. We

may, for example, think of the Flood, of the destruction
of Sodom and Gomorrah, the harassing of Israel by its
enemies, and the destruction of Jerusalem.

2. God wishes these disasters to be a call to repentance,
Luke 13:5.

3. For the Christians, disasters are a chastisement, leading them to stronger faith and a deeper Christian life.
Rom. 8:28; Heb. 12:5, 6. Bearing these points in mind,
the afflictions that come upon nations and individuals
will no longer be a stumbling block to our faith.

GOD'S RELATION TO EVIL-DOING

But our critic charges God with leading David, according to 2 Sam. 24:1, into moral evil, moving him to number
the people of Israel, an undertaking which indeed was
not wrong in itself, but which in this case, it seems, was
begun from motives of pride, conceit, vanity, and thus
became sinful in the sight of God. The statement that
God moved David to commit this sin brings up the old
question what relation the Lord sustains to the many evil
deeds that are performed in the world. It is clear that
He could stop them by the exercise of His almighty
power. It is clear, too, that the people who are trans-
gressing are receiving their life, health, and strength from
God; for, as Paul says, Acts 17:28: "In Him we live and
move and have our being." Is not, then, God responsible
for the many evil deeds perpetrated in the world? For
us nearsighted mortals, who merely know in part, 1 Cor.
13:9, and whose vision cannot penetrate into the mysteries of God's counsels, who cannot grasp the relation
between divine power, providence, and omniscience on

the one hand and man's responsibility on the other, it is befitting that we here exercise a reverential reserve and restraint and do not engage in idle and too easily impious speculations. God has revealed some things to us, and these we must gratefully take as our guide.

In the first place, we can be sure that God does not approve of any wrongdoing, whatever the endowments and powers which He bestows upon the transgressor may be. Just as little as a pious smith approves of the murder committed with the ax which he has forged, does God take pleasure in the wicked deeds done by the arm which He has created and which He supplies with blood and strength. That God frowns on wrongdoing is clear not only from the Ten Commandments, but from explicit statements like Ps. 5:4: "Thou art not a God that hath pleasure in wickedness, neither shall evil dwell with Thee."

In the second place, since men, in spite of God's stern prohibitions and penalties, will do wrong, He uses their evil acts to accomplish His great purposes. The government of a state does not want men to commit theft or arson, as its laws show; but since people will commit these crimes, it uses the convicted and imprisoned criminals, if this is feasible, to do some work that is beneficial to society, as road building. How wrong and silly for anybody to argue that the government encourages crime in order to have a number of convicts whom it can use for construction work! That God in a similar way employs the evil deeds of men to accomplish His gracious designs we see, for instance, from the story of Joseph. Cf. Gen. 50:20. An example of a still higher kind we have in the speech of Caiaphas, who urged that Jesus be put to death, but in his blasphemous language, without knowing it, uttered the central truth of the Gospel, the doctrine of the substitutionary sacrifice of Christ. Cf. John 11:49-52.

SINS PUNISHED BY SINS

In the third place, one particular use which God frequently makes of the wicked acts of men is that He lets one sin be punished by another. The capture of Jerusalem by Nebuchadnezzar was accompanied by revolting acts of wanton cruelty. This was a punishment which God permitted to fall upon Jerusalem on account of its apostasy and wickedness, 2 Kings 24:2 ff. In the passage to which our critic draws attention, 2 Sam. 24:1, a case of this nature is referred to: Israel has sinned, and now God permits its king to become a haughty transgressor, whose evil course calls forth divine punishment. A striking passage confirming this view we have in Rom. 1:26, where Paul says that on account of their idolatry God gave up the heathen unto vile affections, their moral degradation serving as the fitting penalty for their rejection of the true God. Do we not see this truth confirmed every day? The drunkard becomes more deeply entangled in wrongdoing, so that he probably soon finds himself on the gallows. The petty thief becomes a robber and has to be imprisoned or executed as a menace to society, etc.

In the fourth place, I have several times used the term "permit" in speaking of God's relation to sinful deeds. 2 Sam. 24:1, however, says that God *moved* David and said to him: "Go, number Israel and Judah." It might seem, then, that it is not sufficient to say merely that God permits wicked acts to be done, but that we ought to say that in certain instances He *causes* them to be done. The proper view of the matter comes before us when we compare Rom. 1:26, 28 with a parallel passage, Eph. 4:19. In the Romans passage the Apostle says: "God gave them [the heathen] up unto vile affections," and again: "He gave them over to a reprobate mind." In the Ephesians passage, referring to the same people, he says: "Who, being past feeling, have *given themselves* over unto lasciviousness," etc. In the latter passage, it will be observed, the heathen are the ones to whom the giving over is ascribed. The conclusion we reach when comparing these statements is that the heathen were madly rushing into the service of sin, not heeding the admonitions and warning of God, and that, to punish them when His pleadings were disregarded, He withdrew the restraints which He had placed about them and suffered their wicked passions to run their evil course unhindered. It is, then, perfectly right to say that the statement "God moved David to number Israel" means God permitted David to be moved to do such numbering. And who was it that actually and positively influenced David? 1 Chron. 21:1 (the passage our critic assumes to be due to a later development of religious ideas) tells us: "And Satan stood up against Israel and provoked David to number Israel."

In justification of the above explanation I may point to the Sixth Petition of the Lord's Prayer: "And lead us not into temptation," which is best interpreted as is done by Luther: "God indeed tempts no one; but we pray in this

petition that God would guard and keep us, so that the
devil, the world, and our flesh may not deceive us nor
seduce us into misbelief, despair, and other great shame
and vice." Haley, in discussing this matter, says (*Alleged
Discrepancies,* p. 333): "It is consistent with Hebrew
modes of thought that whatever occurs in the world under the overruling providence of God, whatever He suffers to take place, should be attributed to His agency.
In not preventing, as He might have done, its occurrence,
He is viewed as in some sense bringing about the event."
To this ought to be added the thought that God at times
removes restraining influences provided by His mercy
when people in spite of His earnest pleadings eagerly
fling themselves into a life of sin. Every candid reader
will admit, I think, that this interpretation is not putting
too big a strain on human language, but can be justified
by our present-day usage. We say, for instance, of a
board of aldermen which has too radically reduced the
police force that it is responsible for, or is the cause of,
the prevalence of crime in their city. There is, of course,
this profound difference between this action and that of
our great God in the cases under consideration, that He is
meting out punishment and doing it designedly, while
the aldermen are influenced by financial reasons, and the
unfortunate result is not what they had intended. But
the example shows that our human speech uses the terms
"author," "cause," "responsibility," in various ways and
that hence Scripture passages like 2 Sam. 24:1 do not
compel us to look upon our great and holy God as the
author of evil.

Finally, in many a case God will not permit evil deeds

to be consummated. Pharaoh sought to force Israel to return to Egypt; but God interfered, and the design of the Egyptians was frustrated. Saul sought the life of David; God did not permit him to carry out his murderous plans. The enemies of Paul plotted to kill him in Damascus and Jerusalem; but God so guided affairs that their attempts were in vain. In like manner God today, even though one crime wave after the other hurls itself upon us, controls the lives and deeds of men, and many a criminal undertaking does not progress beyond the first stage, that of being conceived and planned.

DESTRUCTION OF THE CANAANITES

There are several other passages which enemies of the Bible like to fasten on when they charge the Old Testament with picturing God as cruel and vindictive. Prominent among them is the command of God given to Joshua and the children of Israel to exterminate the Canaanites. Deut. 20:16-18 we read: "But of the cities of these people which the Lord thy God doth give thee for an inheritance thou shalt save alive nothing that breatheth. But thou shalt utterly destroy them, namely, the Hittites, and the Amorites, the Canaanites, and the Perizzites, the Hivites, and the Jebusites, as the Lord, thy God, hath commanded thee, that they teach you not to do after all their abominations which they have done unto their gods; so should ye sin against the Lord, your God."

Not wishing to repeat what I wrote on this subject elsewhere (*Does the Bible Contradict Itself*, p. 96 ff.), let me merely say that the Canaanite tribes by their shameless vices had filled the cup of their guilt to over-

flowing. When the punishment came, it struck all the
inhabitants, the women and children included. The fault
was not God's; but it lay with those who had trampled
under foot the laws of justice and decency. When men
betake themselves and their families aboard a ship,
sail out upon the ocean for a pleasure trip, and make
that ship a place reeking with wickedness and vice, and
then all perish in a hurricane which suddenly falls upon
them, who is to blame? Will you accuse God for not
discriminating between the adults and the children?
One dreadful aspect of sin is that the woe it produces is
like a whirlpool, whose suction draws every object which
is near by to the bottom. The only difference between
the disaster resulting from the present-day hurricane that
wipes out a wicked city and the extermination of the
Canaanites is that in the latter instance God definitely
announced why He sent such suffering upon those people, while in the case of hurricanes happening today we
have nothing but the general pronouncements of God to
point to in explaining the disaster. That the Canaanitish
women were dissolute and instrumental in causing the
Israelites to leave the path of truth and purity, that for
the children it was better to perish in infancy than to
grow up as devotees of idolatry and of vice, are points
the mere mention of which will suffice here.

THE SO-CALLED IMPRECATORY PSALMS

Closely related to the passages which we discussed in
the preceding paragraphs are the psalms in which God is
implored to send calamities upon the wicked or in which
the writer wishes evil to those that harass and persecute

him. It is said that these psalms are altogether contrary to the spirit of Christ, who has told us to love our enemies, to bless them that curse us, to do good to them that hate us, and to pray for them that despitefully use and persecute us, Matt. 5:45. Even mature Christians will inquire why it is that such passages are found in our Bible.

Among the psalms that come under this head is Ps. 35, some of the verses of which I shall here quote. V. 4: "Let them be confounded and put to shame that seek after my soul; let them be turned back and brought to confusion that devise my hurt." V. 6: "Let their way be dark and slippery, and let the Angel of the Lord persecute them." V. 8: "Let destruction come upon him at unawares, and let his net that he hath hid catch himself; into that very destruction let him fall." Ps. 83 has a few verses of this nature. Vv. 13-17: "O my God, make them like a wheel, as the stubble before the wind. As the fire burneth a weed and as the flame setteth the mountains on fire, so persecute them with Thy tempest and make them afraid with Thy storm. Fill their faces with shame that they may seek Thy name, O Lord. Let them be confounded and troubled forever; yea, let them be put to shame and perish." Perhaps the best-known example of this kind we have in Ps. 137, a song of the deepest pathos, the two last verses of which read: "O daughter of Babylon, who art to be destroyed, happy shall he be that rewardeth thee as thou hast served us. Happy shall he be that taketh and dasheth thy little ones against the stones." The passages cited are typical. We need not here quote others. If it will be found after due considera-

tion of all facts involved that these passages are not contradicting the doctrine of the inspiration of the Scriptures, all others of a like character can easily be defended, too.

One thing that strikes us at once when we read these
psalms is that the author (or his people) has suffered
or is suffering grievously from persecution which is
brought upon him by cruel, merciless enemies. These
psalms are not productions of a diseased fancy which
revels in lurid descriptions of misery and distress; but
they refer to definite historical situations which meant op-
pression and heartache to the author. Again, it is pointed
out in a number of these songs that the wrongs com-
plained of were inflicted by the enemies *without cause.*
The persecutors had been treated with kindness, and
now they requite this benevolence and charity with un-
provoked enmity and wanton cruelty. These are facts
which must not be overlooked.

It will be said, however, that these facts do not justify
any one in hurling maledictions at wrongdoers, and
we have to admit that innocence of wrongdoing when
one is subjected to suffering does not warrant the em-
ployment of abusive, imprecatory terms against the foe.
But these passages, so terrible in their denunciations, take
on an altogether different aspect when we remember
that it is the Lord who is speaking them, even though the
sacred penmen were not mere machines, but voiced their
own sentiments. What we have here is the announce-
ment of the judgments of God upon evildoers. We might
call it the Law in its most terrifying aspect. The same
stern, dreadful truth which God states when He says

in a general way: "Cursed be he that confirmeth not all the words of this Law to do them," is expressed here with specific reference to a certain sinner or sinners. If we have to admit that the Law with its severe, prostrating pronouncements is not foreign to the character of God as it is revealed to us in the Holy Scriptures, then these imprecatory psalms, directed, as they are, against vile transgressors of the Law of God, can no longer be declared unworthy of a place in God's Holy Book. Viewed in this light, Ps. 137:8, 9 gets to be a prophecy of the terrible punishment which was to come upon Babylon, a prophecy which was fulfilled in the course of time.

No Personal Hatred Expressed

But the rejoinder will be made that what is so offensive in these passages is not the prediction of dire punishment, but the sentiment portrayed, namely, the ardent wish, expressing itself in prayer, that calamities and destruction may overtake the enemies, a wish which is held to be incompatible with the love for one's persecutors inculcated elsewhere in the Scriptures, and especially in the New Testament; for, after all, as has been admitted above, though these words have been given by divine inspiration, it is the Psalmist himself who is speaking, his feelings and emotions are depicted. Let us frankly face this difficulty. If the Psalmist here speaks in vindictiveness, with feelings of revenge in his heart, wishing ill to his tormentors in the spirit of hatred, we cannot shield him against the charge of having violated the holy Law of God, among whose unalterable precepts is the lofty rule quoted above: "Love your enemies," etc. But is there anything in these passages which shows that they proceed from a heart filled with hatred and a desire for revenge? I fail to find evidence making such an assumption unavoidable. Harsh language is used, that is true; but there is nothing here compelling us to say that it was dictated by emotions which violate the law of brotherly love. The judge on the bench employs stern expressions when he condemns the criminal. As you have hurt innocent people, so shall you be hurt now, he says in effect. But to infer from this that he is a hardhearted, unloving man would evidently be unwarranted. We must say, on the contrary, that the Psalmist may personally have entertained the kindliest feelings toward his enemies, wishing to see them turn to God in true repentance and obtain divine forgiveness.

If anyone is disposed to deny that these feelings can dwell in the human heart simultaneously with harsh language on the lips, let him think of the stern passage 1 Cor. 5:3-5, where Paul says that he is determined to turn the incestuous person who was besmirching the good name of the church of Corinth over to Satan for the destruction of the body in order that the spirit might be saved in the day of the Lord Jesus. It is evident that Paul is very indignant and aroused, and his language would now be called extremely harsh. But note the feeling of sympathy and love he exhibits toward this sinning member of the church. Though Paul tells the congregation it must expel this man, 1 Cor. 5:13, and though he is willing to give Satan a free hand in afflicting the offender in his body, he is anxious to see his spirit saved. We may safely assume that such were the feelings of the Psalmist when he thought of his enemies.

Let us not make the mistake of thinking that in the Old Testament times the law of brotherly love was not known and inculcated and that Jesus was the first one who taught it. That is a fatal error for the proper understanding of the Scriptures. If the reader will turn to Lev. 19:17, 18, where hatred and revenge are forbidden and the principle of brotherly love is laid down, he will see that we are here speaking of a precept which was contained in the oldest inspired law books of Israel. The Psalmist knew the Law of Jehovah; hence he was acquainted with this principle, too. We must not assume that he would utter any sentiments which were in disagreement with God's revealed will. It is, then, a perfectly justified view if we say his words must not be interpreted as indicative of feelings of revenge and hatred which he harbored, but rather as expressing horror and disgust with respect to evil deeds of which he was the victim.

In addition, it must not be overlooked that the Psalmist in some of the passages under consideration is complaining of wrongs done to God's people, the children of Israel, and that these people at the time were the guardians of divine truth as revealed in the oral preaching and in the writings of the prophets. Any affront against Israel was really an inimical act against Jehovah Himself and His Word. If Ps. 137, for instance, seems so extravagant in its expressions of wrath against those who are molesting Israel and who wish it ill, let us remember that the cause of Israel was bound up with that of divine revelation. We are deeply agitated when anybody insults the American flag, because it symbolizes to us the country of which we are citizens and which we love. Similarly, to the Psalmist, anyone who insulted and hurt Israel was by that token setting himself in opposition to the one true God and to His revealed truth. If so many people nowadays find the language of the psalms we are discussing strange and offensive, it is largely due to indifference toward the sacred teachings which God has given us in His Word.

THE SINS OF THE SAINTS OF THE BIBLE

Every Bible reader knows that the men of God whom we read about in our Holy Book are not pictured to us as perfect people, possessing the purity of angels, but as fallible human beings, who were subject to weaknesses and imperfections and in some instances fell into shocking sins. The story of David's adultery and murder will at once come to mind. In the New Testament the denial of our Lord on the part of Peter is an instance in point. From these sins and imperfections an argument has been taken against the divine origin of the Bible. It has been said that a book whose chief characters exhibit such glaring faults as do those we meet in the Scriptures cannot have been given by inspiration of God.

To enable us to make a thorough investigation of the merits of this charge, it will be well to see precisely what is meant. The Bible, so its enemies say, speaks, for instance, of David in glowing terms, calling him a man "after God's own heart." And yet it relates that this man committed crimes which should have brought him to the gallows. A book which praises such a person cannot lay claim to having come from the hands of the great God, it is held. In reply we say, this is one of the weakest arguments that have been advanced to discredit the

Bible. In fact, what is meant as an attack turns out to be a powerful argument in defense of the Scriptures. Let us see what an unbiased survey of the facts will lead to.

One thing, it seems, every fair-minded person will have to admit when he reads about the sins of God's people brought before us in the Bible, namely, that the Scriptures are a truthful book. It would have been in the interest of the holy writers when they were handing down the accounts of the ancient leaders to picture them as entirely pure and sinless. Think of the inspired penmen as they wrote about David. He was the hero king of Israel, the pride of his people. To all after-generations he was to be an exemplar after which pious Israelites should pattern. How strong must have been the impulse with all patriots among this people to suppress every mention of the discreditable deeds of so great a man! But the holy writers do not yield to this impulse. With utmost candor they tell about the faults of their renowned hero. This is irrefragable evidence that what they are writing is not fiction, but the truth.

Let the reader think of the many familiar instances in the Bible accounts where great men of God have stumbled or have fallen away for a time. Solomon, the glory of his people, in his old age began to abet idolatry. Jehoshaphat, a most attractive figure, strikes up an alliance with Ahab, the wicked king of the Ten Tribes. In the New Testament the twelve Apostles, the chosen band, are chided repeatedly as men of little faith. James and John are rebuked by Jesus for wishing to call down fire from heaven on the hostile Samaritan village. In the night of terror when Jesus is taken captive all the disciples flee and forsake their Master. In the Corinthian congregation there is an incestuous person. The seven letters in the first three chapters of Revelation point to various sad departures of Christian people from God's holy Word. It all serves to confirm our conviction that the Bible is not falsifying, but relating true history.

This feature of the Bible has another great use: it comforts us with respect to our own foibles, weaknesses, and transgressions. If the Bible characters were all immaculate, free from imperfections and impurity, then we could hardly read about them without being overwhelmed by grief and shame, considering our own numerous and startling shortcomings. But we are shown that the great men of God in ancient times had to pass through the same trials and temptations as we and that they were victims of the same weaknesses as the Christians of today. If they were accepted, then there is hope for us, too, we say.

"Impure" Stories

In speaking of the sins mentioned in the Bible, the criticism is voiced by unbelievers that the Bible contains stories which are so shocking to our moral sensibilities as to make the Book unfit to be read in public and to be placed into the hands of the young and as to preclude the possibility of its having had a divine origin. The late Mayor Gaynor of New York once told of a letter which he had received from an acquaintance when the newspapers had reported that the mayor had presented a Bible to a certain library, where he had looked in vain for the Book of Books. This acquaintance remonstrated with him for placing into the library a book, parts of which he would be loath to read aloud in his family circle. The mayor stated that the premise of the objection was wrong and therefore the conclusion was wrong, too. He pointed out that, though the Bible, being a truthful book, at times speaks of heinous deeds, because men commit heinous deeds, nevertheless, it never discusses crime in such a way as to beget love of crime, but always in such a chaste and stern manner that wrongdoing is reproved and combated. For that reason, so he concluded, he did not mind reading aloud any part of the Scriptures at his fireside. The Bible nowhere puts a halo about crimes and criminals, investing them with a seductive charm, as do many modern books. When it speaks of sin, it describes it in its ugliness, so that disgust and horror enter the heart of the reader. Not once, not for a moment, does it leave the high moral level of stern opposition to unrighteousness in all its forms.

Whether it is wise to read certain chapters of the Scriptures in public assemblies is a question which can be answered only if all the circumstances of the occasion are taken into consideration. Every preacher can think of public meetings where he would not hesitate to read any portion of the Scriptures whatever. Then there are meetings where Christian wisdom counsels that we do not publicly read accounts of shocking, immoral deeds. But certainly from this no argument can be taken against the divine character of the Bible. Dr. Torrey (*Difficulties and Alleged Errors and Contradictions in the Bible,* p. 60) draws a comparison between valuable medical works, which naturally contain many a thing a person would not read to every assembly that can be imagined, and the

Bible, which treats of moral and spiritual diseases. "The Bible," says he, "is in part a book of moral anatomy and spiritual therapeutics, and it would be a great defect in the Book, in fact, an indication that it was not from God, if it did not deal with these frightful facts about man as he is and with the methods of healing for these foul moral diseases."

In conclusion, we may well point to a benefit which the plain speaking of the Bible certainly has conferred on millions of Bible readers. "Beyond a doubt," says Dr. Torrey in the discussion from which I just quoted, "many have been kept back from the practice of these sins by the plain things the Bible has said about them. Many others who had already fallen into these sins have been led by the Bible stories to see their enormity and their frightful consequences and have thus been led to forsake them by what the Bible has said about them. I am not speculating about this, but speak from a large experience with men and women who have been tempted to these sins and have been held back by the Bible utterances regarding them, and also from a large experience with others who had already fallen and who have been lifted up and saved by the truth on these subjects contained in the Bible."

SOME INDIVIDUAL PASSAGES EXAMINED

A number of passages which have been discussed quite thoroughly by a number of Christian authors I shall not dwell on at length. Among them are those that relate how Abraham told the Egyptians that Sarah was his sister, Gen. 12:10 ff., and how his grandson Jacob pretended to be Esau, his elder brother, Gen. 27. To my mind these men of God, while firmly believing in the promises they had received, thought they had to help the cause of God by resorting to tricks and schemes and thus fell into wrongdoing. It shows that they were not yet so strong in their trust in God's power, which triumphs over all difficulties, as they should have been. The deed of Jael, Judg. 4:17 ff., has been severely criticized as an unworthy, treacherous act, because she slew the general of the Canaanites who upon her invitation had sought refuge in her house. In defense of her character it has been said that in all probability, when she invited the enemy of the Israelites to come into her house, she had no thought of taking his life, it being impossible for her to know in advance that Sisera would become her guest and that he would fall asleep, so that she would have an opportunity to slay him. This seems to me a very probable view when all circumstances are considered. What Jael did was due to a glowing enthusiasm for the cause of the Lord and His people. Her motives were pure; otherwise she would not have been praised by the prophetess Deborah.

A few remarks about Num. 31:13 ff. may not be unwelcome. Here we have the story of the punishment which Israel, under the leadership of Moses, meted out to the Midianites, putting to death all males and all women that were not virgins. These people had led Israel astray, and the stern justice of God overtook them. The women had had an important part in making the Israelites transgress the commandments of God, as Moses points out in v. 16. Those who were spared became slaves of the Israelites and were given an opportunity to learn the truth about the great God and His gracious promises. Thus we in this episode have an illustration both of the punitive justice of the Lord and of His great mercy.

THE CASE OF FOREIGN WIVES

In the tenth chapter of the Book of Ezra we read about the putting away of strange wives whom some of the returned Jews had married. It may strike the reader as cruel that the husbands in this case were admonished to put away their wives if they were not of Israelitish descent. Was it right for Ezra to introduce such a stern measure, which must have meant a good deal of heartache? Must we nowadays urge people who have married unbelievers that they separate from them? The marriages in question were a plain transgression of a commandment which God had given to Israel and which He had not revoked, Deut. 7:1-3. The children of Israel had been told: "When the Lord, thy God, shall bring thee into the land whither thou goest to possess it and hath cast out many nations before thee, the Hittites, and the Girgashites, and the Amorites, and the Canaanites, and the Perizzites, and the Hivites, and the Jebusites, seven nations greater and mightier than thou, and when the Lord, thy God, shall deliver them before thee, thou shalt smite them and utterly destroy them; thou shalt make no covenant with them nor show mercy unto them, neither shalt thou make marriages with them. Thy daughter thou shalt not give unto his son, nor his daughter shalt thou take unto thy son." From this it is clear that marriages with heathenish women were illegal, and it was perfectly right to dissolve them. We may assume that the unfortunate women and their children were not mercilessly set adrift, exposed to the danger of perishing from hunger, but that provision was made for their maintenance after they had been separated from God's people. The reason for this strict command of God is added, Deut. 7:4: "For they will turn away thy son from following Me that they may serve other gods; so will the anger of the Lord be kindled against you and destroy thee suddenly." Intermarriage easily leads to indifference, a fact which we observe only too frequently in our own day and age.

If the accusation should be brought against Ezra that he mixed Church and State, insisting that the Scriptures be followed in a matter which at least in part belonged to the sphere of the civil government, we must remember that Israel was a theocracy, where the Bible was the law book according to which all social and political questions were to be decided. With respect to New Testament times the old law given in Deut. 7:1 f. has lost its validity. Even if we had no specific statement in the writings of the Evangelists and Apostles showing that this particular law no longer is binding, we should know that it is not in force for us; for the New Testament informs us, for instance, in the Epistle to the Galatians, that all these old ordinances have been removed with the coming of Christ. Cf. especially Gal. 5:1 ff. But in addition we have a specific pronouncement of St. Paul on this subject, namely, 1 Cor. 7:12 ff., where the believing husband or wife is told not to separate from the unbelieving consort. Hence the passage in Ezra, while reminding us of the danger lurking in mixed marriages, must not be looked upon as making in our days unbelief on the part of husband or wife a justifiable cause for divorce.

SOLOMON'S POLYGAMY

But what are we to think of the case of King Solomon, who, as we are told in 1 Kings 11:3, had a large harem of wives and concubines? Is not marriage to be a union between two persons only? And was not Solomon a prophet of God and even an inspired writer, through whom God gave us several books of the Bible? In discussing the case of this wise king, we must remember how emphatically the Bible points to the universality of sin, making only one exception, namely, that of our adorable Savior Jesus Christ. Solomon, with all his piety and wisdom, was a fallible human being, whom we cannot follow in everything he did. It is very true that marriage was instituted to be a union between one man and one woman, a truth confirmed in the New Testament when Jesus says, Matt. 19:5: "The twain shall be one flesh," and when St. Paul, in enumerating godly qualities which a bishop or pastor must possess, includes the monogamous relation, 1 Tim. 3:2, "the husband of one wife."

Many of the saints of the Old Testament disregarded this truth because they were ignorant of it. Among the people about them they saw polygamy being practiced, and they gradually lost sight of the teaching of God on this point. The Lord permitted them to continue in this error, although by the account which He through Moses gave of the institution of marriage and through a passage like Deut. 17:17 He plainly indicated that polygamy does not have His sanction. God could have interposed some more special legislation, but refrained. It was a situation which, to use the expression of St. Paul, "God winked at." If anybody says that the course of the Lord in this case is an offense to him, he has great need of examining his own heart and conduct and of considering how many things in his own life God mercifully overlooks — errors, weaknesses, imperfections. It is extremely difficult to ovecome the downward pull of one's environment or to rise above the level of the world about us. "Be not conformed to this world," states a divine law binding for men in both dispensations. But how hard a task it is! While condemning polygamy and frankly acknowledging that the saints who practiced it committed a sin, although they did it unwittingly, let us praise the long-suffering of God, who forgives even those errors of which we are not aware and cleanses us from secret faults, Ps. 19:12.

THE LYING SPIRIT SENT BY GOD

A passage which arouses a goodly amount of discussion in Bible classes is 1 Kings 22:19 ff., where the sacred historian relates how a lying spirit had come into the prophets of King Ahab, persuading him to proceed against the Syrians, a campaign in which he lost his life. How must we look upon the statement of v. 23: "Now, therefore, behold, the Lord hath put a lying spirit in the mouth of all these thy prophets"? How can we make this statement, which comes from a prophet of God, agree with the Bible teaching that God is truthful and holy in every respect? A little study will show that there is nothing in this interesting story which is incompatible with the attributes of our great God, blessed forever. Micaiah, a prophet of Jehovah, says: "I saw the Lord sitting on His throne." These words mean that he had a vision in which he beheld the majestic sight mentioned, for God is a spirit and hence invisible to mortal eyes. Here we have the key to the explanation of the whole account. Like so many messages in the writings of the Prophets, this one is given figurative form. God granted Micaiah a symbolical representation of His counsels concerning Ahab. Heaven is likened to an earthly court, where the king is surrounded by his advisers and generals. We might call this whole description an allegorical account of what God was intending to do in Ahab's case.

The facts which Micaiah was told of in the vision, and which he here communicates to Ahab and Jehoshaphat, were briefly the following: 1. The counsel of the prophets urging Ahab to proceed to battle was not from God, but from the devil, the enemy of mankind. 2. Ahab's destruction, however, was determined upon by the Lord, and the campaign against the Syrians was to have a disastrous outcome for the king of Israel. 3. God was using the devil in this instance to accomplish His design, the punishment and downfall of Ahab, who was one of the most wicked kings that disgraced the throne of the ten tribes. We have here the familiar method of God, employing the agencies of evil to punish what is evil. To put it differently, God permitted the devil in this instance to work the harm which he is always intent on accomplishing, but from which he usually is kept by the mighty hand of the Ruler of the universe. There are but few, if any, Bible stories which more vividly portray Satan's constant eagerness to inflict injury and the manner in which God employs the forces of darkness to punish the evildoers.

PART FOUR

Historical Difficulties

In this chapter we are concerned with Scripture passages which here and there are thought to involve a violation of historical truth as it is known from such sources as are available to us. The Bible, telling of events which are distributed over an era covering more than four thousand years, is largely historical. Not only does it narrate the origin of the world and the beginnings of the human race, but, after these matters have briefly been dwelt on, it takes up the story of God's chosen people in Old Testament times and relates, often with much detail, how this people repeatedly fell away from God and, having been punished, returned to the faith of the fathers. The narrative culminates in the story of the coming of the promised Seed, the Redeemer, Jesus Christ, who lived and worked here on earth, and then the founding and spread of the Christian Church through the labors of the Apostles are described. It is very clear, then, that the Bible, in many of its parts, is a historical book, and no one need be surprised that contacts between its narrative and that of contemporaneous or subsequent secular writers of history are numerous.

It may not be superfluous to remind ourselves that the Bible, while treating of historical matters in many of its sections, is not intended to be a textbook of ancient history. Just as little as an author who gives us a book on United States history aims to present the history of the world in such a work, though naturally many a reference pertaining to historical events in European and Asiatic countries finds a place in his narrative, so little is it the purpose of the Bible to be a manual of ancient history from the beginning of the world to the destruction of Jerusalem in 70 A. D. When the sacred writers do touch on matters of historical import, it is always from a special point of view, that of the children of Israel and the Kingdom of God. No one, then, need be startled at finding that Egyptian and Babylonian, not to speak of Greek and Roman, history is treated scantily in the Bible. But, though not a manual of ancient history, the Bible, as the Word of God, must be regarded as absolutely truthful and reliable in everything it says on historical matters.

Thinking of the thousands of historical data which our sacred Book contains, we can confidently say that no error has been proved against it, though the attempt has been made by many of its enemies and lukewarm friends. From the days of Celsus, who attacked the historical reliability of the Bible in the second century of the Christian era, to our own day, when historical criticism has reached a marvelously high degree of development, unbelief has been unable to demonstrate in a single instance that a certain historical statement of the Holy Scriptures must in fairness be called false or erroneous. Where this charge was raised, more complete investigation has frequently confirmed the Biblical account in a striking way. In other instances, where the meagerness of the sources makes absolute confirmation impossible, diligent research has shown that from the point of view of the historian the narrative of our sacred Book may very well be true. The science of archaeology, which has been cultivated with great eagerness and success during the last hundred years or so, has furnished abundant and most valuable testimony to the accuracy of the historical data in the Scriptures. The reader may compare some comparatively recent books, for instance, Barton's *Archaeology and the Bible,* Kyle's *The Deciding Voice of the Monuments,* and Cobern's *The New Archaeological Discoveries and Their Bearing upon the New Testament,* where the pertinent material is collected.

CONCERNING THE CHRONOLOGY OF THE SCRIPTURES

We may begin with a few remarks about the chronology of the Bible. In the margin of many of our English Bibles dates are given stating in which year the respective events occurred. These dates were elaborated by Archbishop Ussher, the great Bible scholar of the seventeenth century, and were first put into the margin of the King James Version in 1701. Every Bible reader therefore must be warned not to look upon these marginal chronological notations as being given by divine inspiration. When Ussher places the creation of the world at 4004 B. C., he does so on the basis of very careful studies, which I do not wish to belittle. But he himself would have been the last one to deny that in spite of all his scholarship he was fallible and that his dating might be wrong.

Another point which must not be overlooked is that the inspired Word very seldom submits summaries, giving the total number of years for longer eras. Ussher tells us that the Flood occurred 1,656 years after the creation of the world, and with little effort every one of us can arrive at the same figure by adding the pertinent numbers in Genesis 5. But it will be observed that the Sacred Record itself does not say the total number of years for this span of time was 1,656. We have a summary in Ex. 12:40, 41, where the length of the sojourn of the children of Israel in Egypt is given as 430 years. Similarly the holy writer tells us in 1 Kings 6:1 that 480 years had elapsed from the Exodus to the beginning of the building of the Temple by Solomon. These latter figures, coming to us in the sacred Word itself, must be carefully distinguished from the results which Ussher and other Bible scholars arrive at in their computations.

Closely allied to the above is another consideration, which must not be overlooked. Ussher, as I mentioned before, arrives at the figure 1,656 in computing the number of years that lay between the creation of the world and the Deluge. From the Flood to the calling of Abraham, so his figures tell us, 427 years elapsed. But now let us remember that he takes the word *begat* in the genealogical tables, Genesis 5 and Genesis 11, in the literal sense. While the method of reckoning which he employs seems to be the natural one, the Bible itself indicates that another method is not out of the question. We have genealogical tables in the Holy Scriptures where the word *begat* (or *bare*) is used in the wider sense, denoting merely ancestry. Such is the case in Matt. 1:8,

where it is said of Joram that he begat Ozias, while we
know from the Old Testament that he was the great-
great-grandfather of Ozias, the names Ahaziah, Joash,
and Amaziah having been omitted. Similarly, in Gen.
46:18 it is stated of Zilpah that she bare sixteen souls
unto Jacob, the list showing that her grandchildren and
great-grandchildren are counted among the sixteen. With
these facts before us, we should, it seems to me, be very
careful in making dogmatic assertions about the number
of years that elapsed between the creation and the Flood
and between the latter event and the calling of Abraham.
Since it is very evident that the Holy Scriptures in genealogical tables at times use the word *begat* in a wider
sense, we should speak of chronological data obtained
from such tables with restraint, avoiding undue positive-
ness. Is there not here a hint for us that we must not
spend too much time and energy on solving so-called
chronological difficulties and on that account treating
with neglect what is of real importance in the Scriptures,
the doctrines of sin and grace, the Law and the Gospel?

"Early" Age of Civilizations

At the same time the considerations which have been
submitted above show us that the Bible has nothing to
fear from the researches of historians and excavators who
claim that as long ago as 4,000 years before Christ a high
state of civilization existed in Egypt and Babylonia. That
they will be able to bring absolute proof for this contention seems doubtful. Their conclusions, in all likelihood,
will always remain a matter of conjecture. But even if
they should succeed in furnishing convincing proof that

the world was created earlier than 4004 B. C., the cause of the Holy Scriptures will not have been hurt, since the Bible, as stated above, does not inform us in which year the great act of creation took place.

With respect to the chronology after the time of the Patriarchs other facts, making absolute certainty in our chronological calculations impossible, enter in, which must not be overlooked. The length of the sojourn of the Israelites in Egypt is said to have been 430 years, Ex. 12:40, 41; but from which point does the sacred narrative reckon? Is it from the time when Abraham first went down into Egypt, Gen. 12:10, or from the year when Joseph was taken there as a slave, Gen. 37:36, or from the entry of Jacob and his whole family into Egypt, Genesis 46? To me it seems best to let the 430 years begin with the last-named event. But in the absence of a specific statement in the Biblical records we have to admit that some other starting point for this period is not excluded and that Ussher is within his rights when he lets this period begin with the covenant which God made with Abraham, according to Genesis 15.

Coming to the times of the Judges, a difficulty the student constructing a chronology for the Bible has to contend with is the fact that several of the oppressions and the judges spoken of in the Book of Judges seemingly were contemporaneous and overlapping. Thus Ehud and Shamgar, of whom we read in Judges 3, need not be thought of as following one upon the other, but as living and working simultaneously, one in the eastern, the other in the western part of Palestine. All of which helps to enforce the caution uttered above, to be sober and humble in announcing the results of our chronological calculations, bearing in mind that in the Scriptures God in His wisdom has withheld from us such information as would make a complete and absolutely certain chronology for the Bible times possible. With these general remarks I shall leave the question of chronology. A few passages which have to do with dates will be touched on in what follows.

THE GREAT NUMBER OF THE ISRAELITES AT THEIR DEPARTURE FROM EGYPT

There are enemies of the Bible who in their efforts to discredit the Sacred Volume make the assertion that the Scriptural account of the number of the Israelites at the time of the Exodus gives a figure which is fabulously high, six hundred thousand without the women and the children, a figure which presupposes a birth rate that is simply staggering. To understand the argumentation of these critics, one must bear in mind the premises from which they start. They are chiefly these: The time of Israel's sojourn in Egypt was that covered by four generations, Gen. 15:16; the number of years was 215; the Israelites who entered Egypt were seventy in number, Gen. 46:8-27, of whom fifty-one were grandsons of Jacob. It is assumed that these fifty-one grandsons formed the first generation. Allowing each one the extraordinary large number of ten sons, we obtain 510 male Israelites for the second generation; continuing this rather fanciful rate of growth, the third generation would be repre-

sented by 5,100 Israelites, and the fourth by 51,000.
It will be seen that in spite of a very liberal method of
reckoning this figure is far, far below 600,000. This will
give the reader a conception of the line of argument followed here by the critics of the Scriptures.

To the superficial investigator it might appear that in
this instance we are confronted with a major difficulty,
which it will be hard to explain satisfactorily. But a little
study will soon dispel the clouds that have gathered over
the texts mentioned. We first turn our attention to Gen.
15:16, where the return of the Israelites to Canaan in the
fourth generation is alluded to. Whatever may be the
meaning of the word *generation* in this passage, the time
encompassed by the four generations was four hundred
years, as v. 13 indicates. Bearing in mind the longevity
of the people of Abraham's day, we shall not find it
strange that generation and century are employed as
equivalent terms. Instead of saying, in the fourth century, the holy writer says, in the fourth generation, the
meaning being, four hundred years later. Here there
meets us quite sharply the assertion that the stay of the
children of Israel in Egypt lasted but 215 years, an assertion which is based on the view that Paul in Gal. 3:17,
when saying that the Law was given 430 years after the
promise, makes the whole period from Abraham to the
Exodus last 430 years, which would leave only 215 years
for the sojourn of Israel in Egypt. But the point from
which Paul reckons need not be the time when the
promise was given to Abraham. (Cf. preceding topic.)
It may very well be the time when Jacob entered Egypt,
on which occasion the Lord once more appeared to him

and renewed His glorious promise as to the future greatness of Israel. That this is the meaning of St. Paul we may infer from Ex. 12:40, where the length of Israel's sojourn in Egypt is given as 430 years.

But is it not true, after all, somebody will probably say, that there were four generations from Levi, the son of Jacob, to Moses? Does not Ex. 6:16 ff. give us this order of descent: Levi, Kohath, Amram, Moses (Aaron)? Yes, it is true, there are only four generations enumerated in the genealogy from Levi to Moses as given in this passage. But this is not absolute proof that there were only four generations in this period. There may have been more links in this chain than are here named, for, as pointed out above, it was not at all uncommon in the Hebrew genealogical tables to omit names which were considered unimportant. The situation then comes to have an altogether different aspect from that with which it is invested by the critics. We have a period of 430 years at our disposal, in which there may have been eight generations, allowing a little more than fifty years for a generation. Asking ourselves whether during this span of years the fifty-one grandsons of Jacob could multiply to become a host 600,000 strong, not counting the women and children, we certainly need not hesitate to answer in the affirmative. Even if we allow, to be conservative, but four sons for each family, the seventh generation would have numbered 835,584 males. Thus the charge that the holy writer is guilty of a palpable error, ascribing an increase in population to Israel which is simply fabulous, collapses when it is examined soberly and without prejudice.

BELSHAZZAR

In the Book of Daniel, which is rich in historical material, we find the remarkable story of King Belshazzar, who at a banquet ridiculed Jehovah, the God of Israel, and who that very night, after a miraculous inscription had appeared on the wall of the banquet hall, was slain. It used to be said by hostile critics that this story contains several errors, one of them being the statement that Belshazzar was king of Babylon at the time when the Medes and Persians captured the city and seized the Babylonian kingdom. Now, it is true, that the old secular writers who have given us an account of the conquest of Babylon by the peoples living east of it have a different name for the last ruler of the Babylonian kingdom, Berosus calling him Nabonid and Herodotus saying it was Labynetus. Here a grave difficulty confronted Biblical scholars, which was seized upon with avidity by enemies of the Scriptures in their endeavors to convict our sacred Book of errors.

The difficulty used to be solved in some quarters by the simple, but justified assumption that the king in question had several names, Belshazzar as well as Nabonid or Labynetus; but archaeological discoveries have shown that the solution is found in a different direction. From inscriptions which have come to light it is clear that Nabonid was king of Babylon at the time, but that he was not in command of the city when it was captured by the Medes and Persians. It was his son, whose name the inscriptions give as Belshazzar, who was charged with the protection of the city and who evidently was associated with his father in governing the kingdom, bear-

ing the royal title as well as his father. That he is called
the son of Nebuchadnezzar (Dan. 5:2) may simply mean
that he was a successor of that mighty king, or it may
refer to actual blood relationship, Belshazzar probably
being descended from Nebuchadnezzar on his mother's
side. The proclamation of Belshazzar (Dan. 5:29) that
Daniel, having manifested supernatural wisdom and insight, was to be the third ruler in the kingdom, agrees
well with the situation as sketched above, Nabonid being
the first and his son the second ruler. It can be positively
asserted that archaeology in this instance has completely
vindicated and confirmed the Biblical account, which for
centuries had been regarded with perplexity by some,
while others had not hesitated to reject it as false.

DARIUS THE MEDIAN

In the same connection we meet a reference to Darius,
the Median, Dan. 5:31, which is baffling to Bible students. From our manuals of ancient history we learn that
it was Cyrus who overthrew the kingdom of the Baby-
lonians and who permitted the Jews to return to their
native land. Darius was the name of several kings of
Persia; but they lived and ruled at a later date. Did
Daniel here fall into an error? There is no need for such
an assumption, which would contradict the inspiration of
his book. It is true that on this subject we do not yet possess as much light as we should desire, but perfectly
plausible and satisfactory conjectures have been pro-
posed which solve the difficulty. I shall mention one explanation, which in my view covers all the known data.
In Dan. 9:1 Darius is called the son of Ahasuerus, of the

seed of the Medes. Who was this Darius, and who was this Ahasuerus? What was their connection with Cyrus, the conqueror of Babylon? Secular historians tell us that Astyages, king of Media, was the grandfather of Cyrus and that this Astyages had a son whose name has been handed down as Cyaxares II, who was the uncle of Cyrus. Philological researches have rendered it likely that Darius is but another name for Cyaxares, the former being a Persian, the latter a Median word, both meaning ruler. The same is true of Ahasuerus (Persian) and Astyages (Median), which are not proper names, but royal titles analogous to Pharaoh, king, president, emperor, etc.

The apparent discrepancy arising from the fact that some accounts say Cyrus captured Babylon, while Daniel says that Darius the Mede took it is removed when we assume that Cyaxares served as a general of Cyrus and was prominent in the capture of Babylon and that to him was entrusted the supervision of the newly conquered territory. Davis's *Bible Dictionary* says of Darius the Mede: "He has not been identified with certainty, but was probably sovereign of the Babylonian empire *ad interim* till Cyrus, who was pressing his conquests, was ready to assume the duties of king of Babylon. . . . Perhaps he was Cyaxares, son and successor of Astyages and father-in-law and uncle of Cyrus (Xenophon, *Cyropaed.* 1, 5; 8, 7); or possibly Ugbaru, governor of Gutium, apparently a province in Western Media or on its borders, who led the detachment of Cyrus's army which captured Babylon, held the city for at least four months till Cyrus arrived, and is spoken of in this connection in a cuneiform inscription as Cyrus's governor."

The above, while it does not by any means present an exhaustive discussion of all questions involved, shows, I hope, that the difficulty confronting us in Dan. 5:31 can be explained and that future excavations and discoveries may dispel every vestige of uncertainty as to the correct view of the situation.

THE CENSUS OF LUKE 2:1-5

In the New Testament perhaps no matter involving a date has been more discussed than the census mentioned Luke 2:1-5. The King James Version here speaks of a taxing being decreed by the emperor, but it is universally recognized that census, or enrollment, made, however, with a view to taxation, would be a better translation of the Greek word in question. Luke is said to have blundered seriously in this account. The errors with which critics charge him are briefly the following: 1. that Augustus ordered a general census of the empire and that a census of Palestine was taken at the time of the birth of Christ; 2. that Cyrenius was governor of Syria when the birth of Jesus occurred, 3. that a Roman emporer ordered the Jews to betake themselves to their native city for the enrollment, it being the Roman custom to register people at the place of their actual residence. These strictures sound formidable enough, it must be admitted. The question is whether they can be proved to be valid.

We begin our investigation with the decree of Augustus referred to by Luke. At once the complaints of historians and scholars like Mommsen and Ramsay confront

us that the history of Augustus is enveloped in much
obscurity and that our knowledge concerning his reign
is not nearly so complete as that of other periods of ancient Roman history. It is true that the secular sources
which are available to us do not speak at all of a general
census ordered by Augustus. But neither do they deny
that a decree for such a census was issued. It is a subject
on which they are silent. Now, since information admit-
tedly is very scanty, leaving us in the dark on many a
question, it is not surprising that no mention is made of
a general census undertaken by Augustus to establish the
extent of his power and resources. Here, then, we are
not facing a great difficulty. The fact that certain documents do not refer to a certain event does not prove that
it did not occur. The argument from silence, as it is
called, usually has but little weight. Plummer, who will
not be accused of too great partiality for the inerrancy
of Luke's narrative, says in his commentary on Luke's
Gospel, speaking of chap. 2:1: "It must be confessed that
no direct evidence of any such decree exists beyond these
statements by Luke and the repetitions of it by Christian
writers; but a variety of items have been collected which
tend to show that a Roman census in Judea at this time,
in accordance with some general instructions given by
Augustus, is not improbable."

But more grave seems the accusation that St. Luke has
entirely misdated the census, that the census of Augustus,
carried out by Cyrenius, occurred ten years after the
birth of Christ and that there was no such undertaking at
the time when Jesus was born. From the works of
Josephus we learn that, when Archelaus, the son of Herod

(Matt. 2:22), had been deposed by the Romans, his lands were annexed to the province of Syria and Cyrenius came "to take an account of their substance" and that the Jews, "although at the beginning they took the report of a taxation heinously," finally submitted and gave an account of their estates (cf. *Antiquities*, 18, 1). It is the same census which Luke speaks of in Acts 5:37, and its date is 6 A. D. Other writers of antiquity, it seems, do not dwell on it. To this census, whose historicity is not doubted, Luke is said to have erroneously referred in his famous statement about the time of the birth of Jesus. But even the casual reader will at once have several objections to register. He will point out that Luke, knowing, as his reference in Acts 5:37 shows, the circumstances of the Judean census of 6 A. D., would not be likely to misdate it by ten years or more. He will furthermore remind himself that Luke, in chap. 2:2, apparently is at pains to differentiate the census mentioned there from the later one, occurring 6 A. D., saying that the census of the time when Jesus was born was the *first* one. From this it seems very plain that no person is justified in accusing Luke of simply misdating the census.

But at the time when Jesus was born, so somebody may object, Herod was the king of the Jews, as is evident, not only from Luke's account, chap. 1:5, but especially from Matt. 2:1 ff. How, then, could Augustus at this period order a census which would affect Palestine? The answer is easily given. While Herod nominally was the ruler of Palestine, in reality he was merely a subject of Rome and occupied the throne by the grace of the Roman emperor. The relations obtaining between the latter and Herod are perhaps best reflected in a letter which Augustus in indignation sent to Herod when he learned that the Jewish king had led an army into Arabia. Josephus (*Antiquities,* 16, 10, 3) says of this letter: "The sum of this epistle was this, that whereas of old he had used him as his friend, he should now use him as his subject." The tone of this letter should effectually silence the objection that Augustus would not in a census of his dominions include the territory over which Herod reigned.

THE REFERENCE TO CYRENIUS

We now come to the charge that St. Luke became guilty of an error in ascribing the governorship of Syria at the time of the birth of Jesus to Cyrenius. That we are here facing a difficulty is undeniable. But it is by no means an insuperable one. Cyrenius (Quirinius, according to the Latin form of the name) is said by Josephus to have been governor of Syria in 6 A. D., when he took the census of the Jews spoken of above. The list of Roman governors of Syria for the last years of the reign of Herod the Great (and it will be remembered that Jesus was born while Herod was still living) does not include Cyrenius. From 9 to 6 B. C. a man by the name of Saturninus was governor of Syria, and from 6 to 3 B. C. Varus occupied this position. Since Herod died in 4 B. C., Jesus must have been born about between 6 and 4 B. C., and if our information as to governors of Syria as just given is correct, Cyrenius was not governor when the Savior appeared. But a glance at the Greek New Testament will convince all who are somewhat acquainted with its language that St. Luke does not say that Cyrenius was governor of Syria at the time. A literal translation of Luke 2:2 reads: "This census took place as the first one, Cyrenius controlling (being at the head of) Syria."

A very plausible solution of our difficulty here suggests itself. While Cyrenius may not have been the titular governor of Syria at this time, it is well possible that he actually administered affairs. From secular historians we learn that Cyrenius was in the East at the time of Varus's governorship, and since he was a military man, while Varus was not, the burden of carrying out the orders of the emperor may have rested chiefly on his shoulders. Though we cannot be absolutely certain that this explanation of Luke 2:2 is the right one, what has been said is sufficient to show that the reference to Cyrenius does not convict Luke of a historical error. After all, we need not prove that our interpretation is the only right one; our task here is to demonstrate that the words of St. Luke do not compel us to assume that he committed a blunder.

With respect to the view that St. Luke is guilty of a misstatement when he says that everybody went to be enrolled, every one to his own city, because the Roman system required people to be registered in the town or city where they lived and not in the ancestral home, not much need be said. The statement of Luke, chap. 2:3, does not have to be understood as referring to the whole world, but can well be taken as bearing on Palestine alone. The question, then, is whether the Romans, contrary to their custom, would conduct an enrollment in Palestine in the manner indicated by St. Luke. Recent papyri finds from the first century A. D. give an affirmative answer. Documents have come to light which show that in Egypt the census was taken by the Romans just as described by our Evangelist. If they did it in Egypt, it is but fair to assume that they adopted this method for Palestine, too. We must remember that the Romans were very shrewd in ruling their colonies and provinces, adapting themselves, as much as safety permitted, to the customs and traditions of the subject peoples. In Palestine the census method handed down from the fathers required that people be entered in the lists in that city which was looked upon as the home of their family. The Romans evidently did not see any reason of state which would compel them to carry out the enrollment in a manner not in keeping with the old customs of the Jews. Here, then, we have a conspicuous instance where archaeology brilliantly vindicates the reliability of the Bible record.

It may not be uninteresting to add that, according to census records found during the recent past and dating back to the early period of the Roman Empire, a census was taken by the Roman emperors every fourteen years, the earliest one of these records coming from 20 A. D. If we count back fourteen years from this date, we arrive at 6 A. D., when the census recorded by Josephus and·in Acts 5:37 was held. Going back another fourteen years, we arrive at 8 B. C. Quite likely it was in this year that the census spoken of in Luke 2:1 ff. was ordered. Its execution in Palestine may have been delayed till 6 or 5 B. C., the lack of means of communication such as we possess today and the newness of the undertaking probably being important factors in causing this delay. We must remember that, since this was the first census, an adequate machinery for the enrollment of all the citizens of the empire was not at hand, but had to be invented and constructed. It is, then, not unreasonable to assume that especially in the provinces several years elapsed before the decree of Augustus was carried out.

THE FIFTEENTH YEAR OF TIBERIUS

To the superficial reader Luke 3:1, when compared with chronological tables, will seem to contain a difficulty. St. Luke here declares that it was in the fifteenth year of Tiberius Caesar when John the Baptist began his remarkable, though brief, career. Turning to the historians of ancient Rome, we find that the year of the death of Augustus and of the accession of Tiberius, his successor, to the throne was 14 A. D. The fifteenth year of Tiberius would then seem to be 29 A. D. But this does not agree with such other data as have been handed down to us. If Jesus was born between 6 and 4 B. C., as has been pointed out in the foregoing, He must have been baptized about 26 A. D., for He was about thirty years old when that event occurred, Luke 3:23. To say that John, who preceded Christ about one half year, did not come before the public till 29, would involve us in what seem to be insurmountable difficulties.

But here, as in so many other cases, a closer study of the situation reveals that the fear the consecrated writer may have lapsed into an error is unfounded. We learn from Roman historians (Tacitus and Suetonius) that Tiberius became the associate of Augustus in 11 or 12 A. D. It may well be that Luke reckons from 11 A. D., and the fifteenth year of Tiberius in that case would refer to 26 A. D., which would agree perfectly with other Biblical notices which have to do with this point.

ANNAS AND CAIAPHAS, HIGH PRIESTS

Perhaps some Bible reader has stopped and wondered at the statement in Luke 3:2 that Annas and Caiaphas were high priests when John entered upon his great mission. The high-priestly office was not simultaneously held by two persons. How strange, then, that Luke mentions two men as high priests for that period! The surprise will disappear when one studies the history of the times. Annas had been high priest from 7 to 14, the Romans having deposed him in the latter year. In spite of having incurred the displeasure of the Roman government, he remained very powerful. A son of Annas was among the high priests that preceded Caiaphas, and four sons of his were among those that followed Caiaphas, the latter himself being the son-in-law of Annas. While these facts alone would suffice to make Annas a force to reckon with as long as he lived, there is the additional consideration that at least many of the Jews would not approve of his being removed from his sacred office by the foreign masters and would continue to address him as high priest. When occasion would arise, he would probably be invited by his son-in-law temporarily to fill the high priestly office.

We may point as something analogous to the custom in vogue among us of addressing a man who has served as governor with this title long after he has ceased to hold this office. While Caiaphas was actually the high priest

during the years of the earthly ministry of our Savior,
Annas continued to be regarded as the one who was the
high priest according to the Law of God. Thus it was
natural for St. Luke to speak of two priests for this
period. The Jew who would have been asked at this
time as to the incumbent of the high-priestly office would
have replied, Caiaphas is the man that wears the high-
priestly garments, but really Annas is our high priest,
whom the Romans deposed, ignoring our sacred ancestral
rules, according to which the high priest serves for life.
The more one probes into St. Luke's narrative, the more
trustworthy and reliable it gets to be.

THEUDAS

In Acts 5:36 we find another statement of St. Luke's
which certain critics, without hesitation, set down as an
error on his part. It is the reference to a brigand or revo-
lutionary by the name of Theudas, who before the days
of the census of 6 A. D. fomented trouble and perished
with his adherents. Critics who here accuse Luke of making a misstatement quote Josephus (*Antiquities*, 20, 5, 1),
according to whose account a certain Theudas arose in
revolt during the procuratorship of Fadus (44—46 A. D.).
Luke, it is alleged, in reporting the speech of Gamaliel,
fell into an anachronism, dating the career of Theudas
too early by about forty years. One at once inquires why
Josephus should be thought to be more reliable than
St. Luke, when the latter has now, especially by the researches of Sir William Ramsay, been shown to be a historian of the very first water. On the other hand, the
famous German scholar Th. Zahn has shown that the

work of Josephus frequently lacks accuracy and that gross misstatements abound in his writings.

There are a number of other considerations, however, which entirely remove the suspicion that St. Luke here has committed a blunder. To begin with, the mere fact that Josephus does not mention this particular Theudas is no proof that St. Luke in Acts 5:36 is not speaking of a historical personage. Again, the years before 6 A. D. and this year itself saw many disturbances in Palestine, as the narrative of Josephus bears out. Theudas may have been one of the unnamed insurrectionists alluded to by this historian. The name Theudas was not an uncommon one; there is no reason why there should not have been a man thus named around 6 A. D. as well as in 45 A. D. Or it may be that Theudas was the second name of a disturber whose misdeeds Josephus has chronicled under a different name. Our attention is especially attracted by a slave called Simon, who at the time of the death of Herod the Great (4 B. C.) attempted to seize control of Palestine (*Antiquities,* 17, 10, 6; *War,* 2, 4, 2), but instead of attaining his objective, came to a miserable end. It is well possible that he originally bore the name Theudas and changed it to the popular name Simon when he came forward with his claims. Let the reader, if he is particularly interested in this question, consult the passages in Josephus which relate to this period, and various possibilities accounting for Gamaliel's reference to Theudas as given in Acts 5:36 will easily suggest themselves.

In concluding this chapter, let me merely say that agreement between the Scripture narrative and well-authenticated secular history at those points where they are in contact is simply overwhelming and must confirm us in the belief that the Bible is truly what it claims to be, the Word of God. Whether we think of the four kings mentioned in the fourteenth chapter of the first book of the Bible, whose historicity has been proved by archaeological discoveries that have been made within recent years, or of the reference to Patmos, which we meet in the last book of the Bible, this island being represented as an abode for prisoners, in which role secular history brings it before us, at every point the truthfulness of our Sacred Volume is either at once apparent or is upheld when we engage in more extensive studies.

PART FIVE

Difficulties from
the Point of View of Science

It may be that in this chapter we are facing what nowadays is held to be the chief consideration why the Bible cannot be regarded as an absolutely reliable and trustworthy book — its alleged disagreement with science. We are told that the Bible represents the world view and the scientific notions of the people that lived two or three thousand years ago, that science has proved these views to be erroneous, and that hence the old belief that the Scriptures are God-given and true in every statement can no longer be held, unless we are ready to say that God is a fallible being, which, of course, would be a contradiction in terms. The convinced Christian, saying to himself, on the one hand, that his God does not lie or make a mistake and, on the other hand, that He in great mercy has given us a perfect revelation of Himself and His works, will retort to the claim mentioned above, Bring your proof! He is willing to have the matter investigated, knowing that the truth has nothing to fear before an impartial examining tribunal. It will be well if I first submit a few remarks of a general nature.

Christians are willing to state that they have the highest regard for true science and its achievements.

What is science? It is the careful systematic study of ourselves and the world about us with such powers of observation as the members of the human race are endowed with and can develop. The true scientist occupies himself with the small and great wonders of the universe that are spread out before us. What a noble task! When we consider that the Psalmist in Psalm 19 speaks of the heavens as declaring the glory of God and of the firmament as showing His handiwork; that the holy writer in Psalm 104 revels in the contemplation of the clouds, the mountains, the valleys, the springs, and the birds which sing among the branches; that our Lord Jesus Christ Himself tells us to consider the lilies how they grow, Matt. 6:28; that Paul and Barnabas tell the people of Lystra, Acts 14:17, of the God who witnessed to Himself by giving rain from heaven and fruitful seasons, then we cannot but say that the study of the world and its phenomena has received divine sanction and deserves to be held in high esteem.

There is a different point of view, from which we arrive at the same result. What we see about us, just like ourselves, owes its existence to the heavenly Father, who by His will has produced the universe and all it contains. Nature, it has been rightly said, is a great book, which God has written for us to read, whether we are looking at a giant redwood tree in California, which probably began growing when David was king of Israel, or at a tiny ant, which with marvelous instinct toils for the welfare of its race, or at an amoeba, visible to us only under the microscope, but a marvelous little being nevertheless, expanding and contracting in its quest for food — in every instance we are tracing the writing of our great God.

Nobody who honors the Father in heaven will feel disposed to belittle the attempts which are made by scientists to read for us the great scroll of Nature, inscribed with characters drawn by the finger of God.

No Contradiction Between Science and the Bible

If what has just been said is true, if nature as well as the Bible is a book given us by our great God, it follows that there can be no contradiction between the messages which they bring to us. The same infallible Author is speaking in both. The messages may be different in content. One may be more elaborate than the other, but that they should be in disagreement with each other is unthinkable. If the scientist reads his text correctly, he will not there find a statement which is at variance with the text of the Bible, read and interpreted correctly. We hear much nowadays about a conflict between science and the Bible. There is no such conflict. Pseudoscience, it is true, may contradict clear statements of the Scriptures, or a false interpretation of Scripture may reject as erroneous some facts which true science has established, but a clash between true science and the Bible is out of the question.

In endeavoring to arrive at, and to maintain, sane views on our subject, one must furthermore not forget that the Bible is not a textbook on science. When it was written by holy men of God through the inspiration of the Holy Ghost, the intention was not to give to the world a book that would inform mankind on astronomy, physics, chemistry, botany, zoology, and the like. Our great God had a far different design when He gave us this Volume. Its purpose, as has been stressed before, is indicated 2 Tim. 3:15-17: "And that from a child thou hast known the Holy Scriptures, which are able to make thee wise unto salvation through faith which is in Christ Jesus. All Scripture is given by inspiration of God and is profitable for doctrine, for reproof, for correction, for instruction in righteousness, that the man of God may be perfect, throughly furnished unto all good works." We may here think likewise of the words of the Savior in John 5:39: "Search the Scriptures; for in them ye think ye have eternal life, and they are they which testify of Me." Our Holy Book is intended to lead us to heaven through creating and sustaining in us faith in Jesus Christ, the only Savior. It is not a textbook at all; it is the bearer of a burning message of the love of God as manifested in the coming and the work of Jesus Christ. That is its chief content; whatever else it contains is subsidiary.

THE WORD OF GOD ALWAYS TRUE

But while we have to emphasize that the Bible was not designed as a guide in botany, biology, etc., we have to declare, too, that, whenever it does touch on matters belonging to the sphere of scientific research, it speaks the truth. Coming from the eternal God, it is perfect in every respect, in its chief message as well as in the setting provided for it. Think of a man who is a teacher of chemistry and an authority in this field. His eminence in the sphere of chemistry certainly does not imply that whenever he makes a pronouncement on French literature it is wrong. He may be well informed in this field, too. Let us not think that because the Bible treats chiefly of matters of the soul and heart, of the invisible world and its blessings, its statements cannot be accepted when it has something to say concerning the material world. Certainly that would be a strange conclusion to draw. The ease with which Paul handled the Hebrew tongue did not argue that he was ignorant of Greek. Let us not be so foolish as to think that, since the Bible treats mainly of our relations to God, all its references to phenomena in the physical world have to be branded as false.

We have to be insistent on this point because the Bible itself teaches that it is without error in every respect. To what has been said on this subject where the infallibility of the Bible was under discussion, I here add a few words. When Jesus says, John 10:35, that the Scripture cannot be broken, He is ascribing perfection to our sacred Book, not merely to a part of it. In His battle with Satan, Jesus appeals to what is written as authoritative, not excepting the parts that treat of material matters. "The Law of the Lord is perfect, converting the soul," says the Psalmist, Ps. 19:7. "The Law of the Lord" is an expression referring not merely to the Ten Commandments and other laws, but to the whole revelation of God as it was in the possession of the Israelites during Old Testament times. Cf. Ps. 1:2; 119:97. We should be ignoring a clear teaching of our sacred Book if we endorsed the view that the Bible, when it speaks of things scientific, is not rising above such erroneous views as obtained when it was written.

When the claim is made that scientific discoveries have proved the Bible a book of errors, let the Christian not be daunted. Whoever builds on the so-called "assured results" of science frequently has to find to his sorrow that he is building on shifting sands. While several decades ago the materialistic philosophy of Herbert Spencer occupied the center of the stage and was considered as giving us the final word on the way the universe functions, it is rapidly being discarded, and the views of men like Sir Arthur Eddington, who advocates a spiritual interpretation of nature, are becoming popular. One system displaces another. We may live to see the day when the theory of evolution, according to which not creation, but gradual development is responsible for the many species of beings on our globe, will collapse and be buried in its own ruins. It cannot be emphasized too often that we have to distinguish between science which presents facts and science which ventures to interpret these facts. The former deserves the name; the latter had better be called speculation, in spite of the superior airs which it gives itself.

THE WORLD VIEW OF THE BIBLE

We are frequently asked, Is not the whole world view which meets us in the Scriptures an antiquated one, long exploded by the researches of scientists? A recent writer, quoted by me before, Prof. W. M. Forrest, says (*Do Fundamentalists Play Fair?* p. 13 f.): "The nature of the Biblical universe is clear and simple — the earth was made as a flat body, whose four corners were supported by pillars going down through the waters that were around it and under it; then a canopy, or firmament, overarched it, with waters pent above it for rain and floods. . . . The firmament was only a little way up and might have been reached from the top of the Tower of Babel if Jehovah had not prevented the completion of that ambitious building." Here we have definite statements, the correctness of which we can examine. They are typical; similar ones we hear almost every day. Let us look at them. Does the Bible say that the earth is made as a flat body? I fail to find in it any statement to that effect. The view mentioned is simply an interpretation which the critic puts on the words of the Scriptures. It is true that in Ps. 136:6 the holy writer sends up praise to our great God, "to Him that stretched out the earth above the waters; for His mercy endureth forever." But would it be fair to conclude from this that the Bible teaches the earth is a flat body and not a sphere? The principle that the connection in which a statement is found must not be ignored here comes into consideration. The passage quoted occurs in a poem, and we know that it is one of the properties of poetry to employ bold figures of speech. Why, then, interpret these words as though no figurative language were involved? Besides, it does require a good deal of boldness, it seems to me, to say that, if any one speaks of the earth as being stretched out above the waters, he evidently looks upon the earth as a plane rather than as a ball. Does that really follow? Does the writer or speaker who designates the section of the United States east of the Rocky Mountains as the Great Plains thereby lay himself open to the charge that he denies the globular form of our earth? No one would be willing to hazard such a ridiculous charge.

To continue, what shall we say of the critic's assertion that the Bible speaks of the four corners of the earth, which, as he apparently wishes to imply, does not agree with the view that the earth is a sphere? It is true, the Bible uses the expression "the four corners of the earth"; for instance, in Is. 11:12 we read that the Lord will "gather together the dispersed of Judah from the four corners of the earth." But we ask, Does this prove that the Scriptures teach the earth is a quadrangular body, with four corners jutting out into space? To one who is not hopelessly entangled in prejudice the term will be equivalent to the four points of the horizon. Evidently we are here dealing with an easily understood figure of speech. To those who are overcritical concerning the reference to the corners of the earth by Isaiah we can point to another statement of the same Prophet, in which he, according to the rules of literalists, is denying that the earth has any corners at all, ascribing to it a circular form, Is. 40:22: "It is He [the Lord] that sitteth upon the circle of the earth." But what folly to assert on the basis of such figurative expressions that the Bible teaches this or that view on a question of astronomical geography! Everybody would stand aghast if a person accused Shelley of making the clouds mount to the sun and the moon when he makes one of them say, the mouthpiece of the whole sisterhood:

> I bind the sun's throne with a burning zone
> And the moon's with a girdle of pearl;
> The volcanoes are dim, and the stars reel and swim,
> When whirlwinds my banner unfurl.

> (*The Cloud*, Stanza 5.)

Why apply canons of criticism to the Bible which every-body brands unfair when employed in the field of secular literature?

PILLARS OF THE EARTH

Our critic, to proceed, says that the Bible lets the four corners of the earth be supported by pillars going down through the waters that are around it and under it. Here, too, he can quote Bible passages to bear out his contention, at least in part. 1 Sam. 2:8, Hannah's hymn of praise, says of our great God: "The pillars of the earth are the Lord's and He hath set the world upon them." While nothing is said here about the pillars going down through the waters that are around and under the earth, pillars of the earth, to be sure, are spoken of, and it is said that the world has been placed upon them. But why does not the critic consider the context? Why does he ignore that these words are part of a hymn which is replete with metaphors and which in poetic language expresses the conviction that God has created and now sustains the universe? To anyone who is worried by the thought that the Bible here is actually teaching the existence of colossal pillars on which the globe is resting we can quote Job 26:7, where in words wonderfully sublime the sacred writer says: "He [the Lord] stretcheth out the north over the empty place and hangeth the earth upon nothing." Let no one say that these passages are contradictory. In bold, but beautiful imagery both exalt the infinite power of our great God, in whom we live and move and have our being.

The critic furthermore seems offended at what is said in Gen. 1:6-8 and other passages about the firmament above the earth. Why? we ask. The Hebrew word in question signifies expanse. We today speak of the firmament, or the heavens above us, referring to the sky or the atmosphere. Perhaps our critic's chief difficulty lies in the reference to the waters above the firmament, Gen. 1:7, which, it is true, have been a puzzle to many Bible readers. But how simple is the solution when we think of the clouds and other less concentrated vapors floating far above the earth as the waters above the firmament! On this point F. Bettex, in his little book *The First Page of the Bible,* says (p. 27 of the English translation): "What is the use of this atmosphere, or 'firmament,' as the Bible calls it? we may ask. In the first place, it is to separate the waters above, that is, the clouds, from the waters below. Were it not there, the mass of water which floats above us would as a dense, impenetrable fog hover over the face of the earth and the sea, and groping about in it, we would gain a knowledge neither of the starry heavens nor of the earth's surface, and indeed our whole intellectual life would be destroyed. In this condition it would be ever moist and cold, so that the ripening of the grain and of the fruit would be impossible. But you may think those few clouds above are hardly worthy of being called 'waters above' compared with the immense oceans. However, in this you are mistaken; and were you to live in countries where during the greater part of the year incessant streams fall from above, you would get a different conception of the immense amount of water that is stored up in the sky." This, it seems, should satisfy those who are looking for an explanation of Gen. 1:6-8.

There remains in our little study of the strictures contained in Professor Forrest's words quoted above the assertion that according to the view of the Biblical writers the firmament is only a little way up and might have been reached from the top of the Tower of Babel if the latter had attained the height intended for it. Is our critic serious? we are constrained to inquire. It is true, we read in Genesis 11 that the people who lived immediately after the Flood, having settled in the land of Shinar, said to each other: "Go to, let us build us a city and a tower whose top may reach unto heaven." Is there anything so very strange in this? We call our high buildings skyscrapers, which terms the Germans have translated *Wolkenkratzer* (cloud-scrapers). Is there much difference between the boastful language of the early inhabitants of Babel and our own terminology? They employed an expression which they probably knew well enough to be an exaggeration, and it is not so much their language as the spirit in which they spoke that condemned them. To sum up, if no better arguments against the world view of the Bible can be presented than those just looked at, the Bible has little to fear on this score.

The truth of the matter is, the Bible speaks of the great facts of the physical universe only in a general way. It has some very important things to tell us about the world in which we live, things which science cannot acquaint us with. What I have in mind here is the origin of the world, its preservation, its purpose, its ultimate end. On all these points positive information is granted us in the Scriptures. But when we come to matters like the nature of light, the number of the planets, the law of gravitation, the cellular structure of living beings, etc., it has nothing to say.

That God could have given us authoritative revelations on all the moot questions of science is of course very true. But just as evident is the fact that He did not do it. Does not here the wisdom and love of God manifest itself in a remarkable way? An authoritative book on the wonders and secrets of science — who would have understood it two thousand years ago, when but few instruments or devices were available for accurate and penetrating observation of natural phenomena? Yes, who would understand such a book today? Professor Einstein's theory of relativity is said to be grasped by lamentably few people. Suppose his theory were contained in the Bible, what would be the use? The respective section would be much like the famous mathematical passage in Plato's *Republic* (Sec. 546), which, it seems, nobody today is able to understand. The Bible was written to serve everybody regardless of age or degree of culture; hence we can well understand why the theories and formulae of science are not recorded on its pages.

LANGUAGE OF THE BIBLE POPULAR

While we have to reject the view that our sacred Book reflects the erroneous opinions on scientific matters held by the contemporaries of the Biblical writers, we readily admit, of course, that its language is popular and not that of our modern textbooks of physics and astronomy. Natural phenomena, when alluded to, are spoken of in terms that were current at the time and in the region where the respective Biblical book arose. Just as people today, astronomers included, who hold the Copernican view that the earth revolves around the sun and rotates on its own axis, nevertheless speak of sunrise and sunset, so the Biblical books employ the popular language of their day, which is based on appearance rather than on strict scientific fact. We speak of darkness coming on, just as though darkness were something positive and not simply the absence of light; similarly of death seizing a person and of a drought visiting the countryside. In our everyday speech our eyes catch a glimpse of an object, while in reality the eyes merely receive the picture of an object sent by means of light. Our whole language is permeated with expressions, many of them highly pictorial, built on the appearance of things. Our God through the holy writers addresses us in our own language, so that we may understand Him. Naturally, the peculiarities and idioms of our own speech are not avoided. This accounts for what we call the anthropomorphisms (expressions in which God is spoken of as if He had a human body) and anthropopathisms (expressions which apparently ascribe changeable human emotions to God) of the Bible as well as for its employing the everyday speech of finite human beings in references to the physical world about us.

I emphatically reject, then, the statements of modern critics that the Bible teaches an outmoded view of the universe. Such an assumption is simply incompatible with the conviction that the Bible comes from the great God, who is "the Father of lights, with whom is no variableness neither shadow of turning," James 1:17. Whatever the Bible says, no matter what the subject may be, is true. But at the same time I would warn the reader against making hasty inferences from figurative expressions or popular descriptive phrases current in the language of the day when the Bible was written and universally used to designate certain physical phenomena in an attempt to show what the Bible teaches as to the mechanism of our world. Just as little as Gen. 8:21 is to be taken literally, when Moses says: "The Lord smelled a sweet savor," so little must the following words, found likewise in the account of the Flood, Gen. 7:11: "The windows of heaven were opened," be interpreted to teach that the sky is a solid roof with windows inserted here and there. I cannot approve of the principles of interpretation which, on the basis of the Psalmist's allusion to "wings of the wind," Ps. 104:3, would attribute to the Bible the teaching that the wind is a being equipped with wings.

The world view taught in the Scriptures, as intimated before, has to do with other things than those that scientists dwell on. Not physical phenomena *per se* (taken by themselves), but the divine power manifesting itself in them is the theme. The holy writers do not wish to teach us the number of miles around the earth, but they urge all men to consider the question expressed in these grand words of Isaiah (chap. 40:12): "Who hath measured the waters in the hollow of his hand, and meted out heaven with the span, and comprehended the dust of the earth in a measure, and weighed the mountains in scales and the hills in a balance?" The aims of the Bible, let us not forget, are not intellectual, but spiritual. What it says about the universe is meant to teach us lessons which we need for our soul. Where this is borne in mind, there will not be much danger of a person's becoming over-literal in interpreting the Scriptures.

THE CREATION OF THE WORLD
Genesis 1

The first chapter of the Bible has for many a decade been the battleground of Christians who have striven to uphold the authority of the Scriptures and of unbelievers who have endeavored to destroy that authority by means of ammunition taken from the arsenal of science. I shall here confine myself chiefly to a few general remarks. We cannot approach this chapter without a feeling of deep awe when our God Himself affords us, as it were, a glimpse into His workshop. As He relates what He did at the beginning, let us adore Him, remembering our own insignificance. To all of the attacks made upon the account of Creation as presented by Moses the Christian can reply, in the first place, that the pronouncement of his God on the origin of the world is more important to him than the dicta of scientists. In the second place, he can draw attention to the obvious fact that none of the critics was present when the universe was created, so that he could observe that stupendous event, but that all the critics have to say on this subject rests on inferences, a circumstance which ought to make them very modest in offering their opinions, to say the least. In the third place, the Christian can tell the critics that they cannot be aware of all the gigantic forces, the catastrophes and upheavals, which the Creator may have employed to give our earth its present form. How idle, then, to pay much attention to the so-called verdict of geological strata! Let the strata be studied by all means, but let us here as elsewhere beware of confusing investigation and interpretation.

When the assertion is made that what Moses relates is utterly inconsistent with the evolution theory, which is widely taught these days, we admit, of course, the justice of the remark. But we maintain that the evolution theory, which teaches a gradual ascent of living beings by means of development from lower to higher forms of life, man being the crown of this upward movement, is altogether unproved. It has been well said that Darwin, in his book *The Origin of Species*, has much to say about species, but little about the *origin* of species. There is no evidence to show that one species arises out of another, a lower one; rather, there are facts which decidedly speak against such an assumption. The matter cannot be discussed more fully here. Let the reader who wishes to study the subject from the point of view of the Bible Christian consult books like *Evolution*, by Th. Graebner, *The Problem of Origins*, by L. S. Keyser, and *The Truth about Evolution*, by W. Schoeler.

It is true, skeptics say at every step of the Biblical narrative that what is related is too naive to be true. But they are unable to disprove any part of the account. It must suffice if I dwell on only one point. How could there be light before the creation of the sun? is one question which frequently is asked. The reply is simple. If the theory as to the nature of light which is still widely accepted is correct, according to which light consists in the movements of waves of that mysterious something called ether, there is no reason why there should not have been light before there were great luminaries. On this subject F. Bettex says (*The First Page of the Bible,* p. 24): "Light and the sun are not one and the same. Who has not read of the magnificent aurora borealis? So also comets shine by their own light; and astronomers know of gigantic stretches of light-giving, nebulous matter in the heavens, hundreds of millions times larger in size than our own earth, as, for example, the nebula of Orion. There are now many extinct suns and many others which are invisible to us, so that light without our own sun is clearly possible. And should God will, it is possible for Him to fill the whole universe with an atmosphere, or 'ether,' of the brightest light." In a similar way the other statements in the account which are criticized will, when carefully examined, be found not to contain insuperable difficulties. The story will remain full of miracles, but nothing will appear in it that contradicts established facts.

THE DELUGE
Genesis 6—8

What the Bible tells us about the Great Flood, which destroyed mankind with the exception of Noah and his family, has often been objected to on the ground that it is out of harmony with scientific views. The representation of the Flood as a universal one is attacked, and certain details are objected to, such as the gathering of pairs of animals from all over the earth in Noah's ark to keep the various species from becoming extinct. In beginning our examination of alleged difficulties in this narrative,

let me say that Bible Christians, of course, admit that
the account of the Flood contains many features which
we have to class as miraculous, that is, as things which
we cannot understand. But for the Christian his inability
to explain an event the account of which is contained in
what he has found to be the revelation of God is not
sufficient ground to reject the narrative as untrustworthy.
He knows his God performs miracles, and it is just as
easy for Him to work a million of them as one.

That in the hoary past a great flood occurred on earth
is not denied by critics. The evidence for it is simply
overwhelming. On the one hand, we have traditions
among many nations which distinctly assert that such
a flood took place. Those who have studied the Roman
poet Ovid in their high school or college days will probably remember that in his book called *Metamorphoses*
he has given an interesting and picturesque description
of a terrible flood which brought destruction upon the
whole human race except two people. Here we have
vivid statements like the following: "Spreading far and
wide, the floods rush through the open fields, and together with the crops they carry off groves and cattle
and men and houses and the shrines with their sacred
contents. If perchance a house remained and could
withstand this destruction without falling, still higher
waters would nevertheless cover its gables, and even the
towers were hidden, submerged under the whirlpools.
And soon land and sea no longer could be distinguished.
The ocean occupied everything, and the vast sea was
without a shore." The source from which Ovid obtained
the material for his account of the Great Flood was

Greek literature, where, a number of centuries before his days, without influence known as having come from the Bible, the Flood was dwelt on as a great fact in the early history of mankind.

Since stories of this nature, as has been said, exist with many peoples, the conclusion is inevitable that a flood occurred, the memory of which was preserved in traditions handed down from one generation to the other. On the other hand, we have the testimony of the surface of the earth witnessing to the occurrence of a great flood in the distant past. On high mountains in various parts of the world traces of such a visitation are plainly discernible. Very recently the interest of everybody who reads papers and magazines was challenged by reports coming from Mesopotamia saying that excavators had come upon a stratum of earth which evidently had been caused by a great flood and that underneath this layer of earth they had found traces of an early civilization, utensils, bricks, and pots of a kind not found above said layer. The excavators assert that evidently this stratum marked the end of an epoch in the history of the race. With evidence of this kind before us, it is impossible for anybody to deny the occurrence of a great flood which proved destructive to mankind.

MAGNITUDE OF THE FLOOD

Having emphasized this point, let us now turn to the Biblical narrative itself. It is held that Moses erred when he described the Great Flood as universal. Gen. 7:19 the sacred narrative says: "And the waters prevailed exceedingly upon the earth, and all the high hills that were under the whole heaven were covered." In v. 21 of the same chapter we read: "And all flesh died that moved upon the earth, both of fowl and of cattle and of beast and of every creeping thing that creepeth upon the earth and every man." Vv. 22 and 23 are similar in content. That here the powers of imagination are baffled we have to admit. But who are we to deny or to doubt that God could do exactly what is related in the sacred narrative? It is asserted that the laws of hydrostatics would have been violated by the accumulation of such a great mass of water. This argument is not impressive. The God who created the waters could very well manipulate them, too, in such a way that the results spoken of in Genesis 7 would follow.

When it is stated that the geological strata as they are found today contradict the occurrence of a world-wide flood in historic times, we reply that no man knows what conditions obtained at that time and what forces were at work in the different parts of the world, some here, others there, constituting probably a great diversity of factors, which, while operating simultaneously, naturally did not leave the same traces. In speaking of the Deluge, we do not merely have to think of tremendous rains, but we must also remember that the sacred account itself, in referring to the fountains of the great deep which opened at this time, seems to be pointing to earthquakes as occurring when the great visitation descended upon the earth. Some commentators think that the masses of water necessary to cover the whole earth would have been too vast to let us entertain the thought that such an occurrence actually happened. But considering that three fourths of the earth's surface is water and that the almighty arm of our God could easily hurl these tremendous masses of water upon the mainland, there is nothing in these arguments that the child of God will find disturbing.

Dr. M. G. Kyle, the famous archaeologist, writing in *Bibliotheca Sacra* for October, 1930, connects the account of the Flood with the theories of geologists on the so-called glacial period. He assumes that the pressure of ice on the North American continent was so immense that finally this continent "sank under it. The gorge of the Hudson River shows that at that point the depression was three thousand feet. The rock bottom of the channel is clearly marked right out into the Atlantic Ocean, as soundings have shown. Now, when an elastic ball is pressed in on one side, it bulges out somewhere else; the readjustment must equal the displacement. As the pressure on the land which had caused it to go down had been taken from the ocean, causing a disturbance of the equilibrium there, the bottom of the ocean came up, too, and restored the equilibrium of pressure. 'The fountains of the great deep were broken up'; the water of the ocean was thus thrust right out from the land. This it was which caused the inundation to take place so quickly. The great deposits of loess, deposit of ocean slime, in the Gobi Desert, the great central plain of Asia, is probably the result of that outflow from the breaking up of the fountains of the great deep. Another result took place also at once. The lower edge of the glacier was, of course, at the point where the sun and ice were in conflict. The ice extended as far as the sun would permit it. Thus there would be great fogs along the edge; the atmosphere was overloaded with moisture. The incoming of the great wave of ocean water condensed the atmosphere, and at once 'the windows of heaven were opened,' and the rains came. This was the secondary natural cause of the Flood."

While there is no way of proving that Dr. Kyle's theory as to the cause of the Great Flood is correct, it is interesting and will probably help one or the other of us in defending the Biblical account against the attacks of unbelievers.

THE PLAGUES OF EGYPT AND THE PASSAGE THROUGH THE RED SEA

It was a remarkable series of impressive miracles which God performed when the time had come to take His people out of the house of bondage, which miracles are reported in the Book of Exodus. With respect to the plagues with which God afflicted the Egyptians when they refused to release Israel, it has been said that their miraculous aspects "may be legendary heightenings of historical events" (Fosdick, *Modern Use of the Bible,* p. 163). That is the way in which unbelieving scientists view these occurrences. It is true that these plagues in all probability were not visitations of an altogether strange kind, which the Egyptians had never seen before, but afflictions which were wont to occur now and then in that country. Thus even today we are told there are times when frogs come out of the waters of Egypt in such numbers that they constitute a severe visitation.

If anybody on this account should assert that we are

here not dealing with punishments which Jehovah sent upon the recalcitrant Egyptians, but with events as natural as eclipses, and that it was merely superstition which gave a higher significance to the plagues, he overlooks several obvious considerations. One is that these visitations were of unusual severity; another, that they came in close succession; and a third, that they fell upon the land according to the word of the Lord spoken by Moses and Aaron. There were other features connected with these plagues which made them stand out as due to divine visitation. For instance, the final plague did not attack children in general, but merely the first-born. It would soon be noticed that in every house it was the first-born who was smitten, and in this manner everybody was made to see that a special divine punishment had here come upon the nation. In general, it may be remarked, as I have pointed out before, that God in these visitations followed His usual method, according to which He does not work grotesque wonders, performing unnatural things, but employs forces that are at hand and that are operating in their accustomed fashion, to accomplish His design.

When the children of Israel had left Egypt and Pharaoh was pursuing them, God, in rescuing His people, performed another miracle of special interest to scientists, the miracle which is glorified more than any other one in Hebrew literature. He divided the Red Sea and led the Israelites safely to the other side, while Pharaoh and his hosts were destroyed. Here, too, God employed a natural means to achieve His purpose. We read, Ex. 14:21, 22: "Moses stretched out his hand over the sea, and the Lord caused the sea to go back by a strong east wind all that night and made the sea dry land, and the waters were divided. And the children of Israel went into the midst of the sea upon the dry ground; and the waters were a wall unto them on their right hand and on their left." An east wind has to blow and make the bottom of the sea dry enough for passage.

In discussions of the miracle the assertion has frequently been made that an extraordinary ebb set in which made it possible for the Israelites to reach the opposite shore in their flight, their pursuers, who were too late for passage, being overwhelmed by the returning tide. But it is clear that such a view violates the plain words of Holy Scripture, which say that "the waters were a wall unto them [the Israelites] on their right hand and on their left." If merely an unusual ebb had been responsible for the passageway, there would not have been water on both sides. While holding to the principle just enunciated as to the method of God's working His miracles, we must not alter the Scripture account, but leave its sense unimpaired. What particular forces God employed in restraining the waters we do not know, but His Word, telling us that He did separate the waters, is sufficient evidence for believing children of God that the sea was divided in some miraculous way.

THE CONEY AND THE HARE
Lev. 11:5, 6

In this passage, which is taken from the chapter giving the list of the clean and unclean animals, we meet the difficulty that two animals are called ruminants which according to zoology do not belong to this class. Unbelieving critics have not been slow in saying that here Moses is becoming guilty of an undeniable error and that hence the view attributing inerrancy to the Scriptures is untenable. We shall look at these two verses a little more closely. V. 5 reads: "And the coney, because he cheweth the cud, but divideth not the hoof, he is unclean unto you." The law laid down was that animals which both chewed the cud and parted the hoof might be eaten, but those which did merely one or neither of these two things should be considered unclean. The coney is here declared improper food for the Israelites because, though a ruminant and thus meeting one condition, it does not part the hoof. The Hebrew word here translated coney *(shaphan)* does not designate our coney, or rabbit, but the klipdas, or rock badger ("a rabbitlike ungulate mammal," *Standard Dictionary*). V. 6 reads: "The hare, because he cheweth the cud, but divideth not the hoof, he is unclean to you." The word here rendered hare *(arnebheth)* designates the animal which is known to us by this name.

The famous German Biblical scholar Keil says in his commentary on Leviticus: "The hare and hyrax *(klippdachs)* were also unclean because, although they ruminate, they have not cloven hoofs. It is true that modern naturalists affirm that the two latter do not ruminate at all, as they have not the four stomachs that are common to ruminant animals; but they move the jaw sometimes in a manner which looks like ruminating, so that even Linnaeus affirmed that the hare chewed the cud, and Moses followed the popular opinion." A writer in *Hast-*

ings's Dictionary of the Bible, Vol. II (under *hare*) says: "The hare is a rodent and not a ruminant. The statement (Lev. 11:6; Deut. 14:7) that it cheweth the cud is to be taken phenomenally, not scientifically." The Arab of the present day regards it as a ruminant and for that reason eats its flesh. As Tristram well says: "Moses speaks of animals according to appearances, and not with the precision of a comparative anatomist, and his object was to show why the hare should be interdicted, though to all appearance it chewed the cud, namely, because it did not divide the hoof. To have spoken otherwise would have been as unreasonable as to have spoken of the earth's motion instead of sunset and sunrise." We must remember that Moses is here giving to the children of Israel some practical rules which are to guide them in their choice of food. For that reason their own terms and their own descriptions are employed in designating clean and unclean animals. When all this is considered, the difficulty which people have found in these verses must vanish.

JOSHUA BIDDING THE SUN TO STAND STILL

In Josh. 10:12-14 we have one of the most remarkable narratives in all the Scriptures. In the midst of a great, victorious battle against five kings of the Amorites, when the day seemed too short to accomplish the total defeat of the enemy, Joshua commanded the sun and moon to stand still, and we are told that the sun lingered for about a day longer in the heavens before it set, which gave Israel an opportunity of reaping the full benefits of its victory. In a modern version (edited by J. Powis

Smith) our passage is rendered thus: "It was on the day that the Lord put the Amorites at the mercy of the Israelites that Joshua spoke to the Lord and in the presence of Israel said, 'Thou, sun, stop at Gibeon, and thou, moon, at the valley of Aijalon!' So the sun came to a stop and the moon stood still till the nation took vengeance on their foes. (Is this not written in the Book of Jashar?) The sun stood still at the zenith and delayed its setting for about a whole day. Never before or since has there been a day like that when the Lord heeded the cry of a man; for the Lord fought for Israel." A comparison with the King James Version will show that this modern translation does not contain any important departure from the old, familiar rendering. In our discussion we may well retain the version of the King James Bible.

The account speaks indeed of something inexpressibly grand and stupendous — the lengthening of a day by a number of hours at the request of a pious Israelite. Naturally the story is much attacked. Professor Forrest says (*Do Fundamentalists Play Fair?* p. 15): "To stop the sun to help out Joshua would be impossible, as it does not move with reference to the earth; to stop the earth would destroy it and probably dislocate the whole solar system." Dr. Fosdick thinks that the story we are dealing with may be poetry (*Modern Use of the Bible,* p. 163). Bishop Colenso of South Africa, a higher critic in the Anglican Church, who was deposed by his superior on account of his radical stand, wrote: "The miracle of Joshua is the most striking incident of Scrip-

ture and science being at variance." Thus speaks the
unbelieving world.

Believing scholars have given various interpretations
of our passage. One of them stresses that the Hebrew
word translated "stand still" really means to wait, rest,
tarry. According to his view the miracle consisted, not
in the *standing still* of the sun, but in its remaining
visible for twenty-four hours, as is the case at the north
pole one day after the other during the summer. He
adds: "The method by which this was accomplished we
are not told. It might be by a slight dip of the pole or
possibly by a refraction of the rays of light or in other
ways that we cannot conjecture. It certainly would not
necessitate such a crash in the physical universe as ob-
jectors have imagined." (Torrey, *Difficulties in the Bible,*
p. 54.) The celebrated exegete Keil thinks it possible
that the passage merely states God heard Joshua's prayer
not to let the sun go down till Israel had avenged itself
upon its enemies. However, one fails to see how this
view can be brought in agreement with the inspired
narrative.

DIVINE OMNIPOTENCE

It must not be overlooked that the holy writer says:
"Joshua spake to the Lord," v. 12. The general of Israel
turned to God in prayer. His command addressed to the
sun was not the mandate of a haughty potentate, who,
like Xerxes, thought that even the forces of nature ought
to be subject to him, but the utterance of faith, which
trusts that with God nothing is impossible. Full of confidence in God's help and feeling certain that what he
was about to do had divine sanction, he spoke to the sun

and moon, the words amounting to a prayer that God would interrupt or retard the progress of these luminaries and lengthen the day. That the sun and the moon are both spoken of need not cause surprise, for nothing hinders us to assume that both were visible at the time when the prayer was uttered. As to the precise nature of the miracle and the method which God employed to bring it about, it is simply useless to speculate. The sun stood still, and the moon stayed, says the Biblical narrative. That the passage need not be understood to support the so-called Ptolemaic view of the universe, according to which the sun daily moves around the earth, seems so evident for everyone who realizes that the Bible employs popular speech in its narratives that no further remarks on that point have to be added here. Whether what is here referred to was an absolute stopping of the solar mechanism or merely a relative one is an unimportant question. Either one would require the intervention of God's almighty power.

The assertion that a literal interpretation of the narrative assumes an event and a situation which would have involved the destruction of the solar system need not impress a Christian. The God who created this universe is certainly strong and wise enough to change the course of the sun and the stars and the planets as He sees fit. The question is whether or not we are willing wholeheartedly and unreservedly to accept the Bible teaching of God's omnipotence. If the inviolability of the laws of nature is referred to, then let us not forget that it is recognized even in scientific circles that the so-called laws of nature are merely that which is usually happening and that the term does not designate forces which hold absolute sway in the universe. Neither need it impress us when it is asserted that, even if the possibility of such a miracle is granted, probability speaks against it, since it is not God's method to perform miracles which are simply spectacular and not necessary. Who are we that we should pronounce on the question whether a certain miracle is needed in a given situation or not? There was a very good reason, we can be sure, why God chose this method of assisting Israel. It has been pointed out that the worship of the sun and the moon by the Canaanites might have induced God to bring about the utter defeat of these peoples by the agency of their supposed divinities in order to manifest to the world the futility of this as well as of every other form of idolatry. Whether this conjecture is right or not, we can rest assured that some great and benign purposes of our great God were served when He heard the prayer of Joshua.

The book of Jasher (or Jashar), it may be added, seems to have been a collection of poems, to which additions were made as the years went by and in which new events of a striking nature in the history of God's children could be recorded. The meaning of the word Jasher is correctly given in the margin of the Authorized Version as "upright." Besides in our passage this book is referred to in 2 Sam. 1:18. Who is meant by the upright? Perhaps it is a collective term, referring to the God-fearing Israelites whose deeds were recorded in this "Book of the Upright." The episode related in our passage was soon after its occurrence celebrated in a song which at the time of the composition of the Book of Joshua had been incorporated in the Book of Jasher.

THE SHADOW ON THE SUNDIAL OF AHAZ

When Hezekiah was ill, God heard his prayer for deliverance from what seemed to be certain death and graciously gave a sign to him to strengthen his faith in the divine promise that his health would be restored. The episode is related twice in the Scriptures, 2 Kings 20:8-11 and Is. 38:7, 8. The sign which God granted the pious king was a very marvelous one indeed. The shadow indicating the procession of the hours on the sundial which Ahaz had made, instead of moving ahead in its course, was to retreat ten degrees, thus defying, as it were, natural law and giving evidence of the intervention of the mighty Creator. The sign occurred just as predicted. It has been conjectured that the sundial was near the sickroom of King Hezekiah and was situated so that it could be viewed from there and that hence the king with his own eyes observed the miracle which the Lord worked in his behalf.

It will be inquired, What was the nature of the sign which God performed on this occasion? The account in the Second Book of Kings, which is the more detailed one, tells us that the Lord brought the shadow (on the sundial) ten degrees backward. The precise construction of the sundial is not known to us. It may have consisted of a large pillar or obelisk, throwing its shadow on a huge dial, divided into degrees, or steps (the Hebrew word for degrees, translated literally, signifies steps). As the king and his servants watched the sundial on this particular day, they saw the shadow marking the time going in what would be called the wrong direction. The writer does not say that this was due to the movement of the sun. He furnishes no explanation. His account makes it possible to assume that the miracle was confined to what happened on the sundial, God's almighty power making the shadow move in a direction which was opposite to the usual one.

In the account of Isaiah, however, the statement is found: "So the sun returned ten degrees, by which degrees it was gone down." Ten degrees had been traversed. Perhaps the sundial was divided into half-hours. Since noontime ten degrees, that is, ten half-hours, had been covered, which would make the time of the miracle five o'clock in the afternoon. At this point the sun went back ten degrees. Whether this was done at the usual rate or in shorter time is not stated. Many believing Bible teachers hold that Isaiah is not referring to a miracle happening in the firmament, but to a miraculous event which occurred on the sundial. The prominence which is given to the dial and the shadow and the degrees in the account strongly supports this view. Since there is no mention of a lengthening of the day, this seems preferable to the view which understands Isaiah to say that the sun reversed its course and shone ten hours or so longer than usually.

What is important is that we do not deviate from the intended sense of the narrative as far as this can be determined. That God could have made the sun move eastward instead of westward is as certain to the believing Christian as anything can be. If this were the sense of the inspired account, I should not hesitate a minute to accept it as true. But in all candor I have to say that the meaning of the holy writers seems to be that the gracious sign which God granted Hezekiah consisted in a miraculous happening on the sundial of Ahaz. After all, to make the shadow travel contrary to the laws of light was as much an exhibition of omnipotence as would have been a mandate bringing about the retrogression of the sun in its course in the firmament.

THE PROPHET JONAH AND THE GREAT FISH

Perhaps there is no story in the Bible which is more frequently referred to with contemptuous sneers than that of Jonah's being swallowed by a large fish and remaining in the monster three days before the latter surrendered him to the light of day and to safety. The theology of those who in all simplicity adhere to the Scriptures is often termed a "Jonah-and-the-whale" theology. I hope that the readers of this little volume are not influenced by such taunts, which are very cheap and do not prove anything against the truthfulness of the Bible. Some men who do not wish to pose as enemies of the sacred Book call this story an allegory or a parable, which means to say that in their view the miracle related here never occurred, but that we are here dealing with a fictitious narrative, which was invented for teaching purposes.

It may be well if we begin our inquiry at this point, asking ourselves whether it is possible to look upon this story as a parable invented by a prophet or instructor to bring out, or illustrate, some great truth. That the Bible contains many parables is too obvious to require lengthy discussion. The story of the ten servants (Luke 19: 11-27), which on the face of it reads like the account of a historical event, is called a parable, the term implying that the incidents are merely imagined. Is it possible to look upon the story of Jonah as a parable? This must be denied. There are two considerations which exclude such a view. In the first place, the story itself does not in the least indicate that it is the product of someone's fancy or imagination. There is no hint of any sort leading the unbiased reader to believe that he is perusing a parable. From beginning to end the Book of Jonah purports to hand down historical truth. We cannot but conclude that it was the intention of the writer to have its readers look upon what he relates as realities. In the second place, our Lord in the New Testament treats the story of Jonah's extraordinary experience as historical truth. St. Matthew makes Jesus say, chap. 12:40: "For as Jonas was three days and three nights in the whale's belly, so shall the Son of Man be three days and three nights in the heart of the earth." These words of Jesus confirm the historicity of the story of Jonah, and in the light of His clear utterance any attempt to give the Old Testament account the character of a parable or an allegory had better be abandoned.

Objections of the Critics

But now we have to face the great host of critics who exclaim that the story of Jonah, if taken literally, relates a ridiculous impossibility. The argument that is given stress by them is that a whale has so small a gullet that it could not possibly swallow a man. We are told that it lives on small animals like little crustaceans and mollusks, its throat being so narrow that nothing larger than a man's fist can pass it. While this argumentation may seem impressive to some people, the Christian is not worried by it in the least. If God could provide a fish to be at hand when Jonah was thrown into the sea, He could also make its throat large enough to let the body of a man be passed into the monster's stomach. But what is very remarkable is that the objection of the critics rests on an assumption that is altogether false. It is true, the "right whale," also called "whalebone whale," has the throat described, but the sperm whale, or cachalot, has a gullet which, to quote the manager of a whaling station, "can take lumps of food eight feet in diameter."

In a carefully written article, supplied with all required references and published in the *Princeton Theological Review* of October, 1927, Ambrose John Wilson of Oxford, England, has gathered the information which one needs to arrive at correct conclusions in this matter. The words of the whaling-station manager just quoted are taken from his article. We are here told that it is just the cachalot, a sperm whale, which is found in tropical and subtropical waters, though it has been met with as far north as Iceland. As to its swallowing abilities, Mr. Wilson quotes the same man as saying that the largest thing they had found in a whale was "the skeleton of a shark sixteen feet long." The article submits two accounts of men's having been swallowed by the sperm whale. It informs us that this whale "for the most part subsists on the octopus, the bodies of which, far larger than the body of a man, have been found whole in its stomach." The sperm whale, so it says, "swims about with its lower jaw hanging down and its huge gullet gaping like some submarine cavern. Only too easy to be swallowed by it!" It seems, then, that here there is a big enough grave to receive all the taunts and sneers, objections and criticisms, to the effect that a whale has not a big enough gullet to take a man into its stomach. Other writers, I may add, tell us that sharks have been caught of sufficient size to swallow a man. The sacred account with its parallel passage does not say that the animal receiving Jonah was a whale, the King James rendering in Matt. 12:40 being too specific; the Greek word used there merely signifies a sea monster.

But there remains the objection that, even if the physiological peculiarities of the sperm whale (or of some other big sea animal) cannot be appealed to in an effort to make the story of Jonah impossible, it is unlikely that a man could live in such a house of flesh for three days and three nights. If our great God wishes to preserve a man in such a situation, He can well do it, we reply. In addition we can quote Mr. Wilson's article again, which devotes a special section to the question, Could a man live in a whale? We read: "The answer seems to be that he certainly could, though in circumstances of very great discomfort. There would be air to breathe — of a sort. This is necessary to enable the fish to float. The heat would be very oppressive. 104 to 106 degrees Fahrenheit is the opinion of one expert; a provision maintained by his 'blanket' of blubber, 'often many feet in thickness,' which is needed 'to enable him to resist the cold of ocean' and 'keep himself comfortable in all waters, in all seas, times, and tides' . . . but this temperature, though high fever heat to a human being, is not fatal to human life. Again, the gastric juice would be extremely unpleasant, but not deadly. It cannot digest living matter; otherwise it would digest the walls of its own stomach."

The writer then proceeds to tell of two instances where a man was swallowed by a sperm whale and came out alive from his gruesome prison, the one being that of Marshall Jenkins, who is said to have had this extraordinary experience in 1771; the other that of James Bartley, of whom it is reported that in 1891, while taking part in a whaling expedition, he was gulped down by a furious whale who had been harpooned and that on the second day after his imprisonment and the killing of the monster he was found in its stomach in an unconscious condition, but was revived, and after three weeks had regained his health. Mr. Wilson states in the second article, published in the *Princeton Theological Review*, October, 1928, that the reliability of the story of James Bartley has been impugned; but he shows that what has been adduced against it does not amount to disproof. — Whatever view one may take of the stories alluded to, it must be clearly understood that we Christians do not need them in order to accept the account of the Book of Jonah as true. Its credibility for us rests on far higher grounds than such occurrences. But they may help us to stop the mouths of some critics who take huge delight in referring to the story of Jonah as a "good fish story."

NOTE: An interesting discussion of the report given Josh. 10:12 f. is submitted by Im. Velikovsky, *Worlds in Collision*, p. 39 ff. On the scientific data I cannot pass judgment. Cf. also articles by A. W. Brustat in the *American Lutheran*, June and July 1945.

PART SIX

Miscellaneous Passages

THE SERPENT CAUSING THE FALL OF MAN

In the third chapter of the Bible we meet the sad story of how Adam and Eve, having been beguiled by the Tempter, fell into sin, losing the innocence which was theirs when they issued from the hands of the Creator. There are a number of questions which arise in the inquiring reader as he peruses this narrative. One is, How could evil enter the world, which was good, yea, perfect, when the work of creation was completed? Here we face a mystery, baffling to all thinkers, for which we, standing on the Bible, can offer no other explanation than the one given in divine revelation, to wit, that Satan brought sin into the world. If the inquiry is pushed beyond this point and it is asked, How could Satan, who evidently was created as a good being, become perverted and an enemy of God? we are not able to give a solution. It is a question on which God has not thought it necessary to inform us in His holy Word.

Of all the various details of the story, however, there is none which to such an extent elicits inquiry and discussion as the statements pertaining to the serpent. Does Moses here wish to say that the serpent is a rational animal, gifted with human, or more than human, intelligence, having the faculty of speech, and that it, besides, is a wicked, ungodly creature opposing the plans of the Lord and causing enmity between Him and man, His foremost creature on earth? There is hardly one of my readers who has not given these questions some thought. Some scholars have considered it necessary to have recourse to rather fanciful interpretations in order to defend the Scriptures against the charge of investing the serpent with reason and intelligence. There have been men who have made an allegory out of the whole story and have declared the serpent to stand for evil desires arising in man and causing his downfall. The view has been expressed that it represents intelligence devoid of conscience, as we see such intelligence operating in criminals who use all their intellectual powers for furthering their evil purposes and apparently have entirely suppressed the voice of conscience. There is no reason, however, why we should regard this account as an allegory. The story itself does not say that it is not to be taken literally, and there are no other passages in the Scriptures which direct us to give a figurative interpretation. It must be remembered that a deviation from the literal sense is not justified unless the Scriptures themselves prescribe such a course. Bowing to the plain statements of God's holy Word, we must assume that a real serpent was present when the fall of man occurred and that out of its mouth came the words recorded whereby man was induced to become disobedient to God.

Several facts must not be lost sight of as we are pondering this story. The whole account indicates sufficiently that something extraordinary and supernatural occurred when the serpent spoke. In the second chapter of Genesis we are told that Adam gave names to all the beasts of the field and the fowls of the air, but that "there was not found an helpmeet for him." Here we have the declaration that among the beasts there was no fit companion for him. All of them were of an inferior order, not possessing the eminent mental and moral gifts with which he was endowed. The serpent was no exception. It lacked the faculty of speech and reason and moral insight as much as did all the other beasts. Such is the conclusion one arrives at when reading Genesis 2. Coming to the narrative in the next chapter and reading of the serpent's speaking and leading men astray, the reader will feel at once that here a mysterious evil power is beginning to give evidence of its existence of which the Scriptures have not spoken before, and he will see that the serpent was merely the instrument of this evil force. We must recall here, too, that according to Gen. 1:31 "God saw everything that He had made, and, behold, it was very good." The serpent is included in this comprehensive statement. When it is pictured as the tempter, the reader must conclude on the basis of the preceding narrative that the holy writer does not mean to describe the serpent itself as deceiving man, but is speaking of a mysterious somebody or something making use of it.

WHY WAS THE SERPENT USED?

But why, it will be asked, does this evil person or power employ the serpent for its purposes? We have the reply, it seems, in the first verse of Genesis 3: "Now the serpent was more subtile than any beast of the field which the Lord God had made." When Adam and Eve observed the various animals about them, they soon noticed that the serpent was characterized by a remarkable shrewdness or slyness, which could not but deeply impress the person who watched it. It has been conjectured quite plausibly that on account of this remarkable attribute of the serpent, an attribute which made it less amazing that the serpent spoke than if coherent words had come from the mouth of some other animal, just this beast was used by the Tempter in his attack on Adam and Eve. In other passages of the Bible, too, the serpent is pictured as being possessed of shrewdness. We are all acquainted with the admonition of the Savior addressed to His disciples to be "wise as serpents," Matt. 10:16. Here, then, it appears, we have a sufficient explanation of the course the tempting power pursued when it chose the serpent as its instrument.

In the above we have spoken of the Tempter or the tempting power in vague terms. It will be necessary that we inquire whether the revelation of God does not throw some light on the being that made use of the serpent in the Garden of Eden. And here we can say that, while there are not many passages of the Scriptures which allude to this subject, definite information on the enemy responsible for the fall of man is contained in divine revelation. From the Old Testament we learn that besides the holy angels of God there is an evil angel called Satan, that is, the adversary. Cf. Job 1:6 ff. The narrative in the Book of Job does not say when he became an enemy of mankind seeking to lead human beings into sin; it merely states the fact that he delights in doing injury and in seeing people turn against the Creator.

The remarkable story in 1 Kings 22:20 ff. likewise presupposes that in the invisible world there is a being or beings whose aim is to deceive and to work destruction. It is in the New Testament, however, that fuller light is shed on this mysterious subject. In 2 Pet. 2:4 we read: "For if God spared not the angels that sinned, but cast them down to hell and delivered them into chains of darkness to be reserved unto Judgment"; and a parallel passage in the Epistle of Jude, v. 6, says: "And the angels which kept not their first estate, but left their own habitation He hath reserved in everlasting chains under darkness unto the Judgment of the Great Day." From these statements we learn that there were angels who did not remain in the state of righteousness and holiness in which they had been created, but who sinned, leaving their own habitation, the mansions of heaven, and who by God were cast down to hell, being barred forever from the beautiful home which they left. It is here where we have the origin of evil in the universe. One of these fallen angels is Satan, and it was he who employed the serpent in his successful endeavor to lead mankind into sin.

The Dragon of Revelation 20

In making this last assertion, we are not merely depending on our own combination of facts and deductions. In Rev. 12:9 we read this remarkable statement: "The great dragon was cast out, that old serpent called the devil and Satan, which deceiveth the whole world; he was cast out into the earth, and his angels were cast out with him." Cf. also Rev. 20:2. The fact that Satan, or the devil, is here called "that old serpent" makes it certain that it was the devil who led our first parents into disobedience. And when Paul in Rom. 16:20 says: "The God of peace shall bruise Satan under your feet shortly," he is using figurative language, which is taken from the way in which serpents frequently are killed. Evidently Satan is thought of as a noxious reptile, the head of which is crushed by vigorous stamping of the feet. While not mentioning the serpent, Jesus is clearly referring to the sad episode in Eden when He says, John 8:44, to the unbelieving Jews: "Ye are of your father, the devil, and the lusts of your father ye will do. He was a murderer from the beginning and abode not in the truth because there is no truth in him. When he speaketh a lie, he speaketh of his own; for he is a liar and the father of it." The devil, the father of lying — no one can fail to connect the expression with the story related Genesis 3. It is unmistakable that our Lord ascribes the first lie of which the Bible makes mention to the devil. Hence divine revelation, while not entirely removing the veil which for us lies on the fall of man, has lifted it sufficiently to let us catch important glimpses of what occurred in the Garden of Eden.

If anybody should ask why the serpent, if it was the mere tool of Satan and therefore innocent, was cursed, the reply is that this was done to bring home to man the enormity of the wrong that had been committed, a wrong so great that the instrument of sin was branded as such for all time to come. Whenever we see a serpent, we are to be reminded of the woe that came upon the human race through the wiles of the Tempter, whose design, let us remember, still is to work the ruin of human beings. The charge that God was unjust in thus inflicting a penalty on a dumb, innocent creature is easily met. The serpent by no means is conscious of its cursed state; the sentence that was spoken did not render it unhappy or miserable. To speak of injustice here is as much beside the mark as would be the charge that a farmer is unjust toward his horse if he does not provide for it the glittering harness which can be seen on the horses of his neighbor.

On the question whether the serpent, cursed by God "to go on its belly and to eat dust all the days of its life," Gen. 3:14, ever did have a different posture the commentators are not agreed. Some are inclined to think that originally it moved about in an erect attitude, not forming the object of loathing which it now universally is. To me it seems that such a view is not necessarily implied in Gen. 3:14. The curse of God merely makes the serpent odious to us and leads us to regard its method of locomotion as a mark of degradation quite fitting for an animal that had been used by Satan for vile purposes. We may, as something analogous, point to eclipses, which are a natural phenomenon and have occurred since time immemorial. Who would assume that they did not happen before the Prophets and Christ made mention of them as signs containing an important message for men? But though they are what we call natural events, they are given by God the character of signs and for all who accept the Scriptures have this significance. Thus the serpent may have moved on its belly from the beginning, but ever since the curse this mode of locomotion is a stigma, branding it as the instrument of Satan in the temptation.

SATAN IN THE BOOK OF JOB

In the above I have alluded to the very striking description in the Book of Job in which Satan is mentioned as appearing among the sons of God before the Lord. Satan is not formally introduced and described; it is taken for granted that the children of God reading the book have knowledge of his identity. Undoubtedly this was one of the points on which the teachers in Israel instructed the people. The account, however, contains some valuable hints as to Satan's characteristics. We are told that he "goes to and fro in the earth and walks up and down in it," Job 1:7. Evidently he is a restless being, constantly on the lookout for opportunities of carrying out his designs. We furthermore deduce from the narrative that he is a spirit; for the sons of God who are mentioned Job 1:6 must be the holy angels, who came before the Lord to receive their orders and to give reports. We may think of the description given of them Heb. 1:14: "Are they not all ministering spirits, sent forth to minister for them who shall be heirs of salvation?" The whole scene depicted in Job 1:6-12 is something that takes place in the invisible, the spirit, world, and hence the conclusion is inevitable that Satan, too, is a spirit. Again, it is plain that he is intent on doing harm as he moves about in the world. With reference to Job he says, in a complaining way, that God has made a hedge about him, Job 1:10, so that it was impossible to inflict injury on this pious man. The statement is very consoling to us Christians, showing that Satan's power by no means is unlimited, but that, in doing the mischief he delights in, he can go no farther than God permits. While he wishes to use misfortunes and afflictions as a means to induce men "to curse God," Job 1:11, the story shows that he cannot freely determine the magnitude and weight of these trials, but that God remains the Sovereign, who "is faithful and will not suffer you to be tempted above that ye are able," 1 Cor. 10:13.

What has occasioned most inquiry in this narrative probably is the statement that Satan came before the Lord among the sons of God. Does not that imply that Satan entered heaven? How does this agree with his having been cast out forever from the realms of the blessed?

In looking at these questions, let us remember the remark made above that we are here dealing with events in the spirit world, concerning which we have but an inadequate conception, since it lies altogether beyond the sphere of the experience of mortals. The language used is that which we employ in speaking of human rulers and their courts, and we must conclude that in this way we can best be given an idea of what happened. Was there an assembling of spirits? Was there actual speaking? Do spirits speak to each other as we do?

One thing is certain, a communication of thoughts took place between the Lord and Satan. As to the manner in which it was done, we had better not speculate. It must be observed, too, that the narrative does not say that

Satan came before God in heaven. The place where he was when he replied to the questions of God is not mentioned. It is true that Satan's abode after his fall is the abyss, the region of eternal darkness, and the almighty power of God will see to it that he will not escape. But the imprisonment is not so complete as to prevent him from roaming about on earth "like a roaring lion, seeking whom he may devour," 1 Pet. 5:8.

I cannot conclude this brief chapter without saying that what is of chief importance is not ability to answer the questions concerning Satan which our intellect, and especially our curiosity, ask, but an earnest endeavor to heed the warnings of the Holy Scriptures against the temptations which Satan to the end of the world will throw across our path.

THE SORCERERS OF EGYPT

When reading the Book of Exodus, we meet in chaps. 7—9 references to sorcerers of the Egyptians who tried to imitate the miracles which Moses and Aaron performed in the name of Jehovah to prove the authenticity of their message. Perhaps more strange than any other part of this narrative is the paragraph which tells of the sorcerers' throwing down their rods and changing them into serpents. How must these performances be viewed? When the Lord called Moses to go to Pharaoh and to Israel with a special message, He gave him several signs, and one of these consisted in Moses' throwing his rod on the ground and changing it into a serpent, which, however, was again turned into a rod when Moses took it by the tail, Ex. 4:2-5. That we are here dealing with a divine miracle is evident to every one who regards the Bible as the inspired Word of God. But what shall we say when reading that the wise men and the sorcerers, the magicians of the Egyptians, "did in like manner with their enchantments, for they cast down every man his rod, and they became serpents"? Ex. 7:11, 12. Must we conclude that it was through divine power that they gave this exhibition? It is plain that what happened was something supernatural; man does not possess in his own right the ability here spoken of.

The view has been expressed that perhaps the rods of the sorcerers were serpents which had been put into a state of rigidity by their masters and which began to move when they were thrown down on the ground. But such a view does not agree with the plain letter of the sacred story, which says rods were thrown down and became serpents. Again, it is clear that what the sorcerers did was not accomplished through divine power. The Lord would not abet His enemies in their efforts to counteract the influence of His own servants, Moses and Aaron. There remains only the possibility that it was through Satan that the sorcerers accomplished their feats. That it is Satan who operates in cases where opposition to God and His will is accompanied by miraculous performances is evident from 2 Thess. 2:9, where the Scriptures say of the Antichrist that his coming "is after the working of Satan, with all power and signs and lying wonders," the meaning being that Satan is supplying the power for the miraculous signs of the Antichrist. Here we have the key for the supernatural exhibitions which we find in the camps of the heathen and the unbelievers.

Satan is assisting these enemies of God, and with his aid they do things passing human understanding.

It is very true that on this whole subject there rests the veil of deep mystery because God has not given us much instruction on it. Besides, it is difficult for us to determine how far the realm of human power extends and where the sphere which we term supernatural begins. That the human soul with its many faculties has not yet been fully explored will, I think, be granted without debate. There is an occult field suggested by words like hypnotism, somnambulism, clairvoyance, which still lies within the confines of the natural, but concerning which we know little and tampering with which may prove harmful. Recognizing the existence of powers of the human mind which are still partially hidden to us, we must nevertheless say that the sorcerers' tricks in Egypt cannot be traced back to them. Here there was something transcending the remarkable skill of snake charmers, hypnotists, and like cultivators of the obscure and mysterious, and the only adequate explanation is the power of the Prince of Darkness.

The question has been asked whether classification of the sorcerers' achievements as due to the work of the devil and as consisting in actual performances and not merely in deception is not ascribing too much power to him and making him almighty. There is no reason for entertaining such a fear. The Christian knows that Satan is strong, but he knows, too, that God alone is omnipotent. How Satan brought about those marvelous happenings in Egypt we cannot say. He has faculties and means at his command which are beyond our ken; but supernatural deeds need not be looked upon as almighty deeds. When we say that the angels are stronger than we, we do not ascribe almighty power to them. If we adhere to the letter of the Scriptures in explaining the part the sorcerers played as being in reality the work of Satan, avowing, however, our ignorance of the methods or means he employed, we shall be following a safe course. If this story makes the power of the devil appear very formidable, the child of God will find comfort in that part of the narrative which says that Aaron's rod swallowed up the rods of the sorcerers, Ex. 7:12, God manifesting on the spot His superiority to Satan. And the following narrative not only tells of the inability of the magicians to bring forth lice, which compelled them to confess, "This is the finger of God," Ex. 8:19, but when the plague of boils struck the Egyptians, the magicians likewise were among the victims and could not stand before Moses, Ex. 9:11. We are thus shown that, while Satan can do marvelous things, he cannot do all things and cannot successfully contend against God.

THE WITCH OF ENDOR

Who is there among us that has not with feelings of sorrow and pity, and at the same time of awe, read the story found 1 Sam. 28:5-20, telling of Saul's going to Endor, where there was a woman with a familiar spirit through whose intervention he received a prediction from the spirit world of his impending death? A number of matters engage our attention as we launch into a consideration of this account. The Lord no longer was answering the inquiries of Saul because these were not brought before Him in a filial attitude, but with a mind bent on doing evil. The sacred text says, 1 Sam. 28:6: "The Lord answered him not, neither by dreams nor by Urim nor by prophets."

From the stories of Joseph and Pharaoh, Genesis 37 and 41, we learn that God at times gave revelations by means of dreams. Another method which He employed was that of Urim. In connection with the breastplate of the high priest we find Urim and Thummim, which terms in a literal translation mean lights and perfections. Whether these names stand for some special objects which were in the breastplate and were taken out and used after the manner of lots when the will of God was sought, or whether the meaning is that, when the high priest put on the breastplate and prayed to God, a divine revelation was granted him, we cannot determine. The Israelites of the time of Moses and of David and probably of many succeeding generations knew the manner in which Urim and Thummim were employed. We no longer possess this information. Finally, God often made known His will through prophets whom He sent to Israel and its rulers with a message. In view of the disloyalty of Saul, God at this time did not grant him any directions or guidance in one of the ways mentioned.

Thereupon Saul, becoming reckless and desperate, fearing the strong army of the Philistines, asked his servants to lead him to a witch who might put him in touch with a spirit able to tell him what to do. In taking this course, Saul completely reversed himself. In former years he had put to death or banished all witches and wizards in Israel, obeying in this respect the will of God, who had strictly forbidden all sorcery and witchcraft. Now he himself sought to obtain the services of one of these practitioners of the black art. God had given Israel His Word and the priesthood, and frequently He sent prophets, so that all knowledge needed for their welfare could be obtained. To pry into the future through witchcraft or divination was branded as a wicked procedure. In His wise providence the heavenly Father has flung a thick veil over the future, and to try to lift it by unauthorized means is impudent and presumptuous.

Saul, we are told, went to a woman with a familiar spirit. The term calls for an explanation. A familiar spirit, according to the meaning of the English, is one which sustains intimate relations with the person summoning it and is quite ready to come when called to give information. The English rendering "familiar spirit" is not very definite. An exact translation of 1 Sam. 28:7 reads thus: "And Saul said to his servants, Seek me a woman who is lord (or possessor) of a divining spirit, and I shall go to her and inquire of her. And his servants said to him, Behold, at Endor is a woman who is lord (or possessor) of a divining spirit." This translation will, I trust, enable us to understand a little better the Hebrew idiom involved. The view which finds expression in it is that certain people had control of a spirit whom they could call and consult as to the future. With the help of this spirit, as appears from v. 11 of our chapter, the necromancer, it was assumed, could bring up spirits of the departed in whom the inquirer placed special confidence. From all this it is clear that the familiar spirit, wherever it was not simply the creation of imagination or of conscious deception, was the devil. Jehovah, it must be remembered, had strictly forbidden all witch-craft. Wherever it was practiced with the support of the spirit world, it must have been the enemy of God, Satan, that made supernatural phenomena possible.

When Saul had stated his wish and assured the woman of safety, as she would be complying with his request, she asked, "Whom shall I bring up unto thee?" Could she really summon a departed spirit from the regions beyond the grave to appear on earth and subject him to questioning? That she pretended to have this ability is evident, and Saul, we see, had no doubt that her powers in this respect were genuine. He told the woman to bring up Samuel, and at once she engaged in her incan-tations, we may assume. The next thing reported is that, when the woman saw Samuel, she uttered a loud cry and said to the king: "Why hast thou deceived me? For thou art Saul." Having summoned her familiar spirit, that is, the devil, and being now assisted by him, she recognized the identity of the king standing before her. At the same time she saw something that Saul and his com-panions did not see, an apparition called Samuel in the story. The appearance of the visitor from the spirit world was like that which had characterized Samuel during his life, and Saul, hearing the description given by the woman, had no doubt that the old prophet had come. It seems that the king did not see the unearthly visitor. Whether the words of the spirit proceeded out of the mouth of the woman, which I consider probable, or whether the apparition spoke through vocal organs of its own, cannot be determined with certainty. What Saul heard from the spirit was crushing news, announcing the defeat of Israel and the death of Saul and his sons.

Two Views

Among believing scholars we find two views concerning this remarkable event, which, however, agree in the chief point, namely, in the conviction that it was impossible for the witch and for Satan to summon Samuel or any other one of God's servants who had departed this life out of the beyond to render them service. That Satan cannot bring back upon earth the departed saints is implied in Luke 16:22, where the soul of Lazarus is said to be taken into Abraham's bosom, separated by an unbridgeable chasm from the realm of Satan. We may here think also of the words of Jesus spoken to the penitent malefactor, Luke 23:43: "Verily, I say unto thee, Today shalt thou be with Me in paradise." When Stephen was put to death, he prayed: "Lord Jesus, receive my spirit," Acts 7:59. Paul declares that to depart in his case means to be with Christ, which would be far better than the condition he was in here on earth, Phil. 1:23. When we survey these Scripture texts, the conviction inevitably forces itself upon one that God does not permit Satan or his tools to summon the spirits of the believers to obtain information from them. In this both views agree.

There is a difference of opinion, however, on the question whether it was the spirit of Samuel that was seen by the woman or whether what was beheld was Satan himself, who assumed the outward appearance of the great prophet. The Bible students of the Reformation era and the following century were quite unanimous in championing the view that Satan played the role of Samuel, deceiving Saul, who was under the impression that he was in contact with the prophet. They admitted, of course, that the story says Samuel spoke to Saul and that the words of the spirit fit the life and the character of Samuel, but they held it quite natural to assume that the spirit is merely given the name by which it was referred to in the remarks of the woman and that the holy writer does not think it necessary to go beyond this terminology. That the Scriptures in no other narrative relate the appearance of a spirit of the departed to give information on the future and that, furthermore, the Sacred Record emphatically states God was no longer granting communications to Saul — and for that reason it does not seem likely that He would permit Samuel to appear on an occasion where in direct violation of divine will incantations were uttered and a spirit was invoked — are important considerations favoring this view.

On the other hand, there are believing Bible interpreters, most of them of more recent date, who think that it was Samuel himself that came from the spirit world to announce to Saul his doom. While insisting just as strongly as the old interpreters that the witches and Satan are powerless to summon the saints that sleep into the world of the living, they hold that the letter of the narrative plainly points to the appearance of Samuel himself, who, so they explain, was sent by God to make the dire prediction of Saul's defeat and death. They refer to the shriek of the woman, mentioned in v. 12, and interpret it as being due to her surprise when Samuel, whom she had not at all expected, appeared, her plan being simply to pretend getting in touch with the departed while in reality she would be obtaining her answer to Saul's inquiries through the agency of Satan. To show that saints can appear here on earth if God so wills it, the case of Moses and Elijah is pointed to, who appeared to Jesus at the transfiguration and were likewise seen by Peter, James, and John. If one clings to the blessed truth that no amount of satanic influence can carry the departed saints back into the sphere of mortals, their state being a most happy one, where no trouble can harass them, and if one regards the appearance of Samuel as an exceptional instance, brought about entirely by God's intervention, who intended to make an ultimate pronouncement of His wrath against the wicked king and to do it through the same prophet who had previously announced God's anger to the disobedient ruler, there is no valid reason why such a view should be called unscriptural. The words of the spirit "Tomorrow shalt thou and thy sons be with me" in this case refer to the beyond, the world of the dead, which Saul was soon to enter — a view which does not deny that in yonder world God's children dwell in bliss, while the wicked are punished.

THE SLAUGHTER OF BAAL'S PROPHETS

When Elijah, on one of the grand occasions of his life, had received testimony from heaven that his message was true and that Jehovah was the great God who rules the universe, he told the people: "Take the prophets of Baal; let not one of them escape." The sacred nar-

THE DALLAS HILTON

WE INVITE YOU TO THESE FINE HILTON RESTAURANTS
for your enjoyment and convenience

EL CAFETAL		SADDLE'N
GATSBYS	BEEF	SPUR
BICYCLE BAR	BARRON	BARBEQUE

rative continues: "They took them, and Elijah brought them down to the brook Kishon and slew them there," 1 Kings 18:40. The number of prophets who were put to death at this time was considerable; according to 1 Kings 18:19 there were four hundred and fifty of them opposing Elijah on Mount Carmel. This slaughter of the false prophets has in circles where God's Word is despised been called murder. Some people have asked the question whether here the practice to persecute heretics and to put them to death is not given Biblical warrant.

In viewing these questions, we must remember that the ceremonial and civil laws of Moses had not been withdrawn as yet. While in New Testament times they were repealed by God Himself, at the time of Elijah and King Ahab they were binding upon all Israelites. In this Law there were some stern provisions dealing with idolaters. Let the reader open his Bible at Deut. 13: 13-16 and Deut. 17:2-5 and see what punishment God prescribed for those who worshiped false gods. The Law likewise contained severe legislation against false prophets who would seduce Israel to practice idolatry, the penalty being death. Cf. Deut. 13:1-5. When the prophets of Baal were executed, they suffered the punishment which the God-given Law of Israel had fixed. There was at this time no religious liberty in Israel, but the form of government was theocratic, God Himself being the Ruler, the king His Governor, and the Law of Moses the constitution.

It ought to be clear that this incident does not furnish anybody the right in our day to persecute people who are of a different faith from his own. When the New

Testament dispensation came, the old Ceremonial and the Civil Law which God had given through Moses were set aside, as Paul so gloriously declares and proves in his Epistle to the Galatians; see especially Gal. 3:24, 25 and 5:1. That it by no means would be in keeping with the will of God if we today should proceed against false teachers and prophets with fire and sword is apparent from the stern rebuke which Jesus meted out to James and John when they wished to let fire fall on the Samaritan village which had refused to receive Jesus and His disciples. Cf. Luke 9:51-56. The theocracy ceased long ago; there is no longer any nation which can be called God's people in the same sense as applied to Israel in Old Testament times. Now God's children, constituting the spiritual Israel, are found in all parts of the world. It would be wrong to invoke the old Mosaic legislation to guide us in our attitude towards false prophets. That God abhors idolatry and every corruption of His teaching is something which these passages tell us even today; but their direction to put to death those who worship false gods and teach such worship was intended only for the days of the Old Covenant.

If, finally, the question is asked whether Elijah did not transcend the limits of his authority and resort to mob law when he told the people to seize the prophets of Baal, the reply is that he was the special ambassador of God and that, since the civil authorities did not enforce the constitution and stop the heinous transgression of the divine Law which these prophets were guilty of, he, as God's messenger, had to intervene and himself carry out the divine will.

DEMONIAC POSSESSION AT THE TIME
OF CHRIST

Many are the passages of the New Testament which speak of persons who were possessed of devils. Frequently Jesus heals such unfortunates by expelling the demons. Several questions arise in this connection. We inquire, What is meant by demoniac possession? Why were instances of this affliction so frequent in those days? How was it possible for some of the Jews who were not followers of Jesus to practice exorcism, that is, expulsion of demons? As to the precise nature of the state we are speaking of, we must distinguish between being controlled morally and being controlled physically by the devil. Of Judas Iscariot we read, John 13:2: "The devil having now put into the heart of Judas Iscariot, Simon's son, to betray Him" (Jesus), etc., and again in v. 27: "After the sop, Satan entered into him." Luke says likewise, chap. 22:3: "Then entered Satan into Judas, surnamed Iscariot, being of the number of the Twelve." What we are viewing here is the inexpressibly sad condition of a person who is under the moral or spiritual control of Satan, yielding to the evil impulses which Satan arouses in him. When we speak of persons as being possessed by the devil, we do not refer to the service which is rendered Satan by every wicked person, but the term is meant to denote a state in which the person afflicted is physically controlled by the Prince of Darkness. Frequently such possession may have been due to a life of sin; at times, however, as in the case of the boy spoken of Mark 9:14 ff., there may have been no moral depravity on the part of the victims to which the extraordinary power of Satan over them could be attributed.

The persons who were possessed by devils at times, in some cases probably continuously, were not masters of their own bodies, of their limbs and their organs of speech. There were hours when somebody else directed their actions and spoke out of their mouths. The demoniac in the country of the Gadarenes, when asked by Jesus what his name was, replied, "My name is Legion, for we are many," referring to the number of devils who were having their habitation there, Mark 5:9. It was the mouth of the demoniac that was speaking, but the statement that was made came from the devils that were residing in him. We may describe the state of such persons, then, as being that of a dual personality, the victims' own personality now and then becoming entirely submerged and the devil assuming control of all their organs and faculties. A remarkable phenomenon found with persons so possessed was that they through the devil inhabiting them recognized Jesus as the Son of God and hailed Him as such when He came near them. Thus when Jesus entered the synagog at Capernaum, as related Mark 1:23 f., a man with an unclean spirit, that is, a devil, cried out: "Let us alone; what have we to do with Thee, Thou Jesus of Nazareth? Art Thou come to destroy us? I know Thee who Thou art, the Holy One of God." It is plain that here more than human insight was manifesting itself. In such cases Jesus always forbade the spirits to speak, and though the Scriptures do not inform us as to the reason why He took such a course, we can easily find an explanation for it. He did not wish to build His kingdom with the help of Satan, and hence He refused to profit by what the devils could divulge about His person.

In addition to supernatural insight we at times see in the possessed exhibitions of superhuman strength. The demoniac in the country of the Gadarenes had "plucked chains asunder and broken fetters in pieces," Mark 5:4. This confirms the view that here we are dealing with a phenomenon which must be classed as supernatural. I am aware that this is a matter in which great reserve is proper and wise; for who will fix the limits of a person's strength when he is under the influence of great mental stress? But it seems that we are not going too far in describing the strength of this man as superhuman.

DEMONIAC POSSESSION DIFFERENT FROM INSANITY

From the above the reader will see that I reject the view one hears frequently these days that the so-called demoniacs were merely insane and that possession of the devil was a figment of the imagination of the people living in the first century A. D. Such a view cannot be held by those who look upon the Bible as the inerrant Word of God and upon Jesus, who bade the demons depart, as the omniscient Lord. At times it is asserted that Jesus knew quite well that there was no such thing as demoniac possession and that He, in expelling the demons, merely accommodated Himself to the ideas and the language of His contemporaries. But this theory of accommodation ill suits Him who insisted on honesty and sincerity and who used very strong language in dwelling on the hypocrisy of the scribes and Pharisees. How can we assume that He deliberately deceived the people who surrounded Him and were guided by His message? Whether now and then insane persons were mistakenly regarded as possessed of devils is a different question. Quite likely the dividing line between these two states was not always carefully observed. But that there was in those days an affliction which was properly described as possession by evil spirits, Bible Christians must consider incontrovertible.

When we ask why cases of this sad state apparently were very frequent at the time when Jesus visibly moved among men, we are driven to conjectures, because the Scriptures do not furnish us information on this matter. A very plausible explanation is that the devil realized the Redeemer had come for the salvation of the world and the destruction of his kingdom and that hence he made very determined efforts to counteract the work of Jesus and the Apostles, using all means at his command, physical and spiritual, in opposing the coming of the Kingdom of God. The situation is very aptly described in the words of Jesus, Luke 11:21, 22: "When a strong man armed occupies his palace, his goods are in peace; but when a stronger than he shall come upon him and overcome him, he taketh from him all his armor wherein he trusted and divideth his spoils." Warfare was on between Jesus and Satan when the former entered on His work. Satan was aware of the intention with which the Son of God had appeared on earth, to storm the citadel which Satan was occupying. There had to come a gigantic conflict between the Prince of Life and Light and the Prince of Death and Darkness, and demoniac possession was one of the weapons the latter employed in this struggle. Taking this view, we shall not think it strange that cases of this affliction were so frequent in the days of the earthly life of our Savior. There is, of course, no reason why we should hold that demoniac possession cannot occur today; but to enter upon that subject would take us beyond the scope of this book.

JEWISH EXORCISTS

There remains the question how we shall account for it that demons were expelled not only by our Lord and His disciples, but likewise by persons that did not belong to His circle. That such was the case the Bible reader knows from Luke 11:19 and the parallel passages. What is indeed remarkable is that Jesus Himself here acknowledges devils were being ejected by some of the Jews called exorcists. The statement of our Lord is so definite that we cannot describe these persons simply as impostors who were probably enriching themselves at the expense of their credulous countrymen. That a good deal of fraud was practiced under the mantle of exorcism we may readily grant, knowing from our own observations that the occult furnishes quacks of divers descriptions a fruitful field for their attempts to fleece the public. But there must have been some genuine cases of expulsion of demons by exorcists. How could they perform such a thing? Evidently through the power of Jehovah, the true God. We have to think of their endeavors the same way in which we regard the ejection of demons by the apostles. The latter performed this miracle not through their own power, but through the power of God; the genuine exorcists mentioned by Christ did their work in no other way. God was merciful to the distressed and permitted healings to be performed by these men. In all this there is nothing contrary to sound doctrine and true piety.

DID JESUS OPPOSE MARRIAGE?

That is the interpretation that has been put on the words of our Lord in Matt. 19:12. A modern writer, opposing the divine character of the Scriptures, has said: "Jesus taught that marriage was evil; celibacy, a sacred piety; a horrid self-mutilation, a pious, acceptable sacrifice for the kingdom of heaven's sake." In investigating whether these irreverent words correctly state the position taken by Jesus, let us remember that the words alluded to were spoken when He had given information on the question of divorce, laying down the rule that, except when adultery has been committed, a divorce is contrary to the will of God. Over against the loose practice prevailing at the time among the Jews with respect to divorce, Jesus insisted that the marriage bond should be considered indissoluble by husband and wife. Instead of belittling or destroying the sanctity of marriage, He exalted and defended it. No one can truthfully say that the statements of Jesus in Matt. 19:1-12 betoken a low view of the married state.

When the disciples say that, if the marriage vow is binding till death and a husband cannot at will rid himself of an unworthy, troublesome wife, it is not good or profitable to marry, Jesus has a word to say about the unmarried state. Dr. Goodspeed's translation of Matt.

19:10-12 quite well brings out the meaning, and therefore I transcribe it here: "The disciples said to Him, If that is a man's relation to his wife, it is better not to marry. He said to them, It is not everyone who can accept that, but only those who have a special gift; for some are incapable of marriage from their birth, and some have been made so by men, and some have made themselves so for the sake of the kingdom of heaven. Let him accept it who can." The statement of the disciples that, if Jesus has correctly given the meaning of marriage, it is not good or profitable to marry, He takes up for a little more discussion. He does not say that they are wrong, but He asserts that the principle which they have just uttered cannot be accepted and acted upon except by those who have received a special gift from God, referring to the gift of continence. There are three classes of people who refrain from marriage — those who are unfit for it through physical defect, those who have been rendered unfit by cruel mutilation, and those who have made themselves unfit for it for the sake of the kingdom of heaven, that is, who voluntarily, in order to assist more effectively in extending the kingdom of heaven, forego marriage, having been equipped for such a course by a special divine endowment enabling them to remain chaste without the married relation.

In all this there certainly is no condemnation of matrimony. Furthermore, Jesus here does not even advise people to remain unmarried, nor does He say that he who does not marry is manifesting greater godliness and piety than the one who enters upon matrimony. Whoever imputes such sentiments to Jesus is reading things into His words which are not there. His words rather contain the warning: "If you think that for yourself an unmarried life is preferable, be sure that you have the gift of continence." The charge that our Lord is recommending horrid self-mutilation rests on a misapprehension of His words. It entirely ignores the consideration that the statement of Jesus may well be taken in a figurative sense, making oneself a eunuch simply meaning the determination to remain unmarried. In fact, there are strong reasons showing us that in this instance the literal sense must be discarded and a figurative sense adopted. As Luther very acutely remarks: If, in speaking of people of the third class, Jesus likewise referred to self-mutilation, He would be speaking of the same sort of thing as referred to in what He says about people of the second class. Besides, mutilation of one's own body is clearly forbidden in the divine Commandment "Thou shalt not kill" and calls to mind the words found Rom. 1:24, where Paul speaks of men that dishonor their own bodies. It is certain that Jesus would not have commended a course which so plainly runs counter to the revealed moral code.

CAN JESUS BE ACCUSED OF AN OCCASIONAL UNDUE HARSHNESS?

We are all familiar with the strong language which Jesus used against the scribes and Pharisees as reported in Matthew 23, where He denounced them as hypocrites and charged them with various other sins. No Christian holds that Jesus was too vehement in these utterances; for not only do we know that the Savior was sinless, being the Son of God, but that He was dealing with a set of men for most of whom religion had become a matter of outward observance and who, while they were interested in hundreds of little rules of conduct, neglected the chief things in the Law; cf. Matt. 23:23; Luke 11:42.

There is another occasion in the life of Christ where some people think He displayed extraordinary severity. Luke 9:59, 60 we read: "He said unto another, Follow Me; but he said, Lord, suffer me first to go and bury my father. Jesus said unto him, Let the dead bury their dead; but go thou and preach the kingdom of God." A superficial reading creates the impression that Jesus forbade this person attendance at the funeral of his father, who was about to be buried, and that He demanded from him the apparently altogether unnecessary sacrifice of foregoing the highly prized privilege of joining friends and relatives in according his father the last honors. A little reflection and study, however, will show that such a view does not apprehend the real meaning of the passage.

To begin with, the command of Jesus "Follow Me" had the significance, as the present tense of the Greek verb shows, "Be My follower; be My constant companion." What Jesus requests is not that the young man at once forsake all tasks and duties with which he at the moment was confronted, but that he become His disciple and travel about with Him and the Twelve, listening to the instruction of the Master, who had come from God. It was not imperative that this be done the next minute or the next hour. Jesus was satisfied if it was done as soon as possible.

THE YOUNG MAN'S FATHER WAS STILL LIVING

We must furthermore not assume that the father of this young man had died and that the corpse was awaiting burial. If such had been the situation, it is more than doubtful that there would have been any contact between Jesus and him. In Palestine the burial was not performed several days after death had occurred, as is the case with us, but as a rule it took place on the same day on which the person had died. A few hours after the news had spread that a certain member of the community had passed away, the funeral procession would be seen going to the tomb. Bearing this in mind, we have to think of the father of this man as still living, but as being old and near the end of his earthly career, and the son quite naturally expresses the wish to be permitted to stay with the parent as long as the latter was among the living and to attend to the funeral rites, which were regarded as a matter of great importance. Filial respect and love were, and still are, a prominent trait in Oriental countries, in which matter Westerners might well learn a lesson from their fellow men in the East. The son in this case expressed the desire to do what custom and sentiment demanded of him; but Jesus tells him that he must put first things first. God has a higher claim on us than our parents and other relatives. This young man was now called by Christ to take a part in the spreading of the heavenly kingdom, and this call had to be given first consideration. When remembering that Jesus is here not refusing permission to this man to attend the funeral of his father, but is merely telling him that he must not delay entering His service and becoming a minister of the Gospel till the death of his father, the charge of un-natural harshness as made against Jesus collapses.

In this connection the saying of the Lord "Let the dead bury their dead" may be given a little attention. What does the Savior mean when making this utterance, which sounds somewhat obscure? The explanation commonly given seems to be the right one, the words of Jesus hav-ing this significance, Let those who are spiritually dead bury their people who are bodily dead. That is work which they can do and which is in keeping with their character. They cannot be used for the proclamation of the kingdom of God, so let them attend to the funeral of their relatives.

In the same connection (Luke 9:61, 62) another saying of Jesus is reported which is causing difficulty to some people. We read: "And another also said, Lord, I will follow Thee, but let me first go bid them farewell which are at home at my house. And Jesus said unto him, No man having put his hand to the plow and looking back is fit for the Kingdom of God." The superficial reader may think that Jesus here is denying a person the priv-ilege of bidding farewell to his parents and other rela-tives before he starts out on a tour intended to further the spreading of the Kingdom of God. Does not the attitude which the Lord here takes seem unnatural and even inhuman? If the text is carefully scrutinized, the whole difficulty disappears. The man offers himself to Jesus as a disciple and servant, but before joining the Master, he requests to be given the privilege of saying farewell to the members of his family. It will be ob-served that Jesus does not tell him the permission which he asks for cannot be granted. Not one word of that. Whoever interprets this text as saying that Jesus told this man, You must not bid those at your house farewell, is reading something into the passage which is not contained in it. But Jesus issues a warning to this man. When the latter speaks of willingness to follow Jesus, but in the same breath refers to earthly ties that have a claim upon him, it was very proper that the admonition should be given him that whoever wishes to serve Jesus must do it wholeheartedly, placing such ministry higher than everything else here on earth. The words of Jesus, then, tell us that whoever enters the Gospel ministry must know that the service which Jesus wants is not to be a divided service, one half going to the Lord and the other half to persons and objects here on earth. His messengers must enter the work with a devotion to their heavenly Lord which is sincere and complete. The saying of Jesus indeed sounds a very earnest note, but no one can accuse it of manifesting undue harshness, as though it insisted on the smothering of all natural affections.

DOES THE BIBLE INCULCATE HATRED TOWARDS ONE'S RELATIVES?

Quite jubilantly enemies of the Bible wishing to undermine its authority point to Luke 14:26, where Jesus, in discussing the cost of true discipleship, said: "If a man come to Me and hate not his father and mother and wife and children and brethren and sisters, yea, and his own life also, he cannot be My disciple." There our great Master, we are told, demands of His followers that they

hate those who are near and dear to them. What a religion! Who would want to be among its advocates?

Now, such talk does not impress the Christian. He
knows that our Lord taught love, urging His disciples
to love even their most bitter enemies. He thinks likewise of Matt. 15:4, where Jesus emphasizes that the
Commandment "Thou shalt honor thy father and thy
mother" must not be set aside. Whatever may be the
sense of the passage referred to, it cannot be intended
to make us entertain hatred toward our relatives. For
many centuries, disciples of Jesus have been reading
this saying of their Lord, and they have never been led
by it to become neglectful of loving-kindness toward
their family circle. Nor do I know of a single instance
where any one of them was shaken in his faith by what
enemies of the Gospel call a cruel or inhuman saying.
But it is true that one or the other of the followers of
Jesus has found it difficult adequately to explain the
strong language Jesus uses.

To account for the terminology of our Lord, we must
remember that the word *hate* is used in the Scriptures
in the sense of "to love less." We find it thus employed
in Gen. 29:31, where the sacred writer says that the Lord
saw Leah was hated; the preceding verse, however, states
that Jacob loved Rachel more than Leah, from which
we conclude that loving less and hating were terms
which at times were used synonymously. Dr. James Mof-
fatt, in his recent book *Love in the New Testament*
(p. 43), draws attention to this peculiar nomenclature.
Discussing the words of Jesus, "No one can serve two
masters; either he will hate the one and love the other,"

he says: "Here *hate* is a strong term for indifference to the interests of the master, as it is in the claim for exclusive devotion to Christ which may involve in special heroic circumstances that the claims of the family must be set aside: 'If anyone comes to Me and does not hate his father, and mother, and wife, and children, and brothers, and sisters, aye, his own life, he cannot be a disciple of Mine.' The meaning of the words of Jesus, then, simply is that we must love Him more than anybody else, be he ever so dear to us and his claim upon our affection ever so strong. It signifies that, if we have to choose between loyalty to Christ and loyalty to friends and relatives, Christ always must be given the preference. Knowing our proneness to give first place to earthly ties and values, He employs heroic language, as it were, to make us realize the significance of true discipleship, involving, as it does, willingness to suffer for His sake the loss of everything one here cherishes. Plummer, in discussing this passage in his commentary, says that Jesus here, 'as often, states a principle in a startling way and leaves His hearers to find out the qualifications.'" It was not very difficult for them to see what He meant and to harmonize this saying of His with others from His lips in which faithful observance of filial and conjugal duties had been dwelt on.

In the same chapter of Luke's Gospel we find another statement of Jesus which belongs to the class of hard or strong sayings. Vv. 12-14 we read: "Then said He also to him that bade Him, When thou makest a dinner or a supper, call not thy friends nor thy brethren, neither thy kinsmen or thy rich neighbors, lest they also bid thee again and a recompense be made thee. But when thou makest a feast, call the poor, the maimed, the lame, the blind, and thou shalt be blessed; for they cannot recompense thee; for thou shalt be recompensed at the resurrection of the just." Looking at these words of Jesus, the question arises in us, Does the Lord forbid us to invite our friends and relatives to be our guests and enjoy a meal at our table? Is the only kind of hospitality which He sanctions that which we classify as belonging to charity? In opening the discussion, let me say in passing that our Lord certainly would not approve of those orgies of eating and drinking which people are so fond of these days, orgies which show that the attitude of the contemporaries of Noah before the Flood prevails to an alarming extent, when the desire to satisfy one's appetite for delicious food and drink was the ruling passion and, to use the phrase of St. Paul, people made their belly the god whom they worshiped.

ENTERTAINMENT OF FRIENDS NOT FORBIDDEN

But the question confronting us here is whether Jesus opposes innocent gatherings of friends and relatives, where Christian fellowship is enjoyed and our natural affections are afforded an opportunity of asserting themselves. At once the Christian reader will say that Jesus cannot have meant to interdict all entertaining of one's friends, rich neighbors, and relatives, for He Himself at times was the Guest at meals which belonged to this category. The wedding at Cana can be mentioned here, likewise the occasion when He was anointed by Mary, John 12:1-3. Furthermore, when we examine the Greek of the passage, an important consideration presents itself. "Call not in thy friends," says the Savior. The verb in this case is in the present tense, so that the significance is, Do not *always* or regularly or habitually call thy friends. Again, let it be observed that the tenor of the saying is directed, not against hospitality toward one's kin, but against that selfish hospitality which is practiced with the motive of serving one's own earthly interests. The finest exhibitions of friendship are vitiated when they flow from that foul source — selfishness.

An argument advanced by Farrar in his little commentary on St. Luke likewise deserves consideration. He draws attention to passages where similar language is used, a particularly striking one being Matt. 9:13: "I will have mercy and not sacrifice." In this quotation from the Old Testament the Lord must not be understood to say that He is displeased if the Israelites offer sacrifices to Him. As a matter of fact He had on many a page of the Old Testament directed His children to honor Him by sacrificial offerings. But we must remember that the Israelites, when Hosea wrote the words quoted, were in the habit of offering up sacrifices which were an abomination to the Lord because they proceeded not from a heart filled with love and mercy, but were a mere mechanical performance. To express His abhorrence of such rites, God said, "I will have mercy and not sacrifice," the meaning being, I will have mercy by all means and not merely sacrifice. We, then, have a good basis for interpreting the words of Jesus to mean, Do not invite merely your friends and relatives, but invite especially the poor, who cannot requite the good you are doing them. Whoever entertains his friends and wealthy neighbors, who can and will return the favors bestowed on them, must not imagine that he is doing a great, good work. While not forbidden, such a course does not betoken love toward God and one's fellow men. And if it keeps one from engaging in works of mercy, it gets to be positively harmful.

A WORD IN CONCLUSION

Having completed our joint consideration of a number of Scripture passages which are called difficult, I hope the conviction is very strong in my readers that the Bible, after all, is God's Word and that it has nothing to fear from the many attacks which these days are made on it. It has been demonstrated, I trust, that for such difficulties as our limited intelligence and experience find in it plausible explanations can be offered. Wherever the solutions submitted seem insufficient, we can confidently look forward to further research to furnish the desired light, thinking of the many instances in which during the recent past patient study, explorations, and excavations have brought us the knowledge that was needed to remove the clouds obscuring certain texts. With still greater confidence we can fix our expectation on the great school above to dispel whatever difficulties remain for us here and there in the Scriptures. "Now I know in part, but then shall I know even as also I am known," 1 Cor. 13:12.

My prayer is that the attitude of all my readers toward the Scriptures may ever be that which our great God Himself urges us to assume, saying, Is. 66:2: "But to this man will I look, even to him that is poor and of a contrite spirit and *trembleth* at My Word." Trembling at God's Word, sincere reverence, deep humility, may these characteristics be ours when we open the Sacred Volume and meditate on its life-giving contents! A great poet has said that the truth is a torch, but an enormous one, and that those who approach it too closely will be consumed. We may use the same metaphor in speaking of the book of eternal truth, the Bible. It is a gigantic beacon light, sending out helpful rays into the dark world. Those who in all humility are guided by it will reach the true homeland, the city which hath foundations, prepared for us by the love of God and opened to sinners through the blood of the Lamb; but those who neglect its beneficent directions or who in self-willed curiosity and perhaps with feelings of superiority and contempt tamper with its heaven-lit flames will, if they persist in their course, bring destruction upon themselves. Manna from heaven, water springing up into everlasting life, is offered in our Holy Book. Will you, dear reader, not come with a grateful and believing heart and receive these gifts of God?

> How firm a foundation, ye saints of the Lord,
> Is laid for our faith in His excellent Word!
> What more can He say than to you He hath said
> Who unto the Savior for refuge have fled?

Subject Index

171

Index of Passages

NEW TESTAMENT